Job Security in America

Job Security in America
Lessons from Germany

Katharine G. Abraham
and
Susan N. Houseman

The Brookings Institution
Washington, D.C.

Copyright © 1993

THE BROOKINGS INSTITUTION

1775 Massachusetts Avenue, N.W., Washington, D.C. 20036

Library of Congress Cataloging-in-Publication data:

Abraham, Katharine G.
   Job security in America : lessons from Germany / Katharine
G. Abraham and Susan N. Houseman.
      p.   cm.
   Includes bibliographical references and index.
   ISBN 0-8157-0076-8 (alk. paper)—ISBN 0-8157-0075-X
   (pbk. : alk. paper)
   1. Job security—United States. 2. Job security—Germany.
I. Houseman, Susan N,   II. Title.
HD5708.45.U6A27   1993
331.25'96—dc20   92-37545
                                                              CIP

9 8 7 6 5 4 3 2 1

The paper used in this publication meets the minimum
requirements of the American National Standard for
Information Sciences—Permanence of paper for Printed
Library Materials, ANSI Z39.48-1984.

Ⓑ THE BROOKINGS INSTITUTION

The Brookings Institution is an independent organization devoted to nonpartisan research, education, and publication in economics, government, foreign policy, and the social sciences generally. Its principal purposes are to aid the development of sound public policies and to promote public understanding of issues of national importance.

The Institution was founded on December 8, 1927, to merge the activities of the Institute for Government Research, founded in 1916, the Institute of Economics, founded in 1922, and the Robert Brookings Graduate School of Economics and Government, founded in 1924.

The Board of Trustees is responsible for the general administration of the Institution, while the immediate direction of the policies, program, and staff is vested in the President, assisted by an advisory committee of the officers and staff. The by-laws of the Institution state: "It is the function of the Trustees to make possible the conduct of scientific research, and publication, under the most favorable conditions, and to safeguard the independence of the research staff in the pursuit of their studies and in the publication of the results of such studies. It is not a part of their function to determine, control, or influence the conduct of particular investigations or the conclusions reached."

The President bears final responsibility for the decision to publish a manuscript as a Brookings book. In reaching his judgment on the competence, accuracy, and objectivity of each study, the President is advised by the director of the appropriate research program and weighs the views of a panel of expert outside readers who report to him in confidence on the quality of the work. Publication of a work signifies that it is deemed a competent treatment worthy of public consideration but does not imply endorsement of conclusions or recommendations.

The Institution maintains its position of neutrality on issues of public policy in order to safeguard the intellectual freedom of the staff. Hence interpretations or conclusions in Brookings publications should be understood to be solely those of the authors and should not be attributed to the Institution, to its trustees, officers, or other staff members, or to the organizations that support its research.

Foreword

DURING RECESSIONS in the United States, millions of workers are temporarily or permanently laid off from their jobs. These workers typically suffer personal hardships and large income losses. In other industrialized nations, employers are less likely than in the United States to respond to reductions in sales with layoffs. In this study, Katharine G. Abraham and Susan N. Houseman address whether the job security afforded to U.S. workers could be strengthened without harming the competitiveness of U.S. industry.

Abraham and Houseman's analysis rests on a detailed comparison of labor market policies and industrial relations practices in the United States and Germany. Whereas U.S. policies encourage the use of layoffs if employers must reduce employment, German policies foster a mix of work sharing in the short run and reductions in employment through attrition and early retirements over time. In addition, the German apprenticeship system enables workers to move from one task to another. Although German employers are less likely than American employers to lay workers off, they appear able to adjust equally well to changing economic conditions and to distribute the costs of adjustment more evenly across the work force.

The authors argue that, although policies that work well in one country may not work well in another, the German experience contains important lessons for American policymakers. Abraham and Houseman advocate reforms intended to remove the bias of current policy that favors the use of layoffs and discourages the use of work sharing. They also advocate policy changes that would facilitate expanded workplace training in the United States.

Katharine Abraham is a professor of economics at the University of Maryland and a research associate of the National Bureau of Economic Research. Susan Houseman is a senior economist at the W.E. Upjohn Institute for Employment Research. At the time of the project's inception, Abraham was a research associate and Houseman was a guest scholar at the Brookings Institution.

Abraham spent two months as a guest scholar at the Wissenschaftszentrum für Sozialforschung in Berlin. She is grateful to Christoph Büchtemann and Ronald Schettkat for their hospitality during that period. Both authors would like to thank the many employers, employers' association and trade union representatives, government officials, and scholars with whom they met during several subsequent visits to Germany and whose perspectives have helped to shape the conclusions of the present volume.

The authors have also benefited from participation in seminars at Princeton University, the National Bureau of Economic Research, Washington State University, the University of Washington, the University of Delaware, Ohio State University, the Massachusetts Institute of Technology, the Wissenschaftszentrum für Sozialforschung, and the IFO Institut in Munich. The full manuscript was reviewed by Timothy Bartik, Daniel Hamermesh, Paul Osterman, Ronald Schettkat, Robert Spiegelman, and Wayne Vroman. All of them provided valuable comments.

The authors also thank Kelly Eastman, Steve Fagin, Katherine George, Carolyn Thies, and Heidi Wiedenman for research assistance and Claire Vogelsong for her work in the preparation of the manuscript. Theresa Walker edited the manuscript, Roshna Kapadia and Laura Kelly checked it for factual accuracy, and Susan Woollen prepared it for typesetting. Carolyn Thies produced the figures, and Florence Robinson prepared the index.

The Brookings Institution gratefully acknowledges the financial support for this project provided by the Andrew W. Mellon Foundation.

The views expressed in this book are those of the authors and should not be ascribed to those acknowledged above or to the trustees, officers, or staff members of the Brookings Institution.

Bruce K. MacLaury
President

December 1992
Washington, D.C.

Contents

Figures

Job Security in America

CHAPTER ONE

Introduction

Duringa downturn, employers in the United States typically rely heavily on layoffs to trim an excess work force. The mass layoffs of the 1980s and 1990s, however, have spurred worker demands for greater job protection. Concern over worker dislocation in the United States is shown in a number of recent private and public sector initiatives. The prevalence of job security provisions in collective agreements increased substantially during the 1980s.[1] In 1988 Congress passed the first federal legislation requiring employers to notify workers in advance of mass layoffs or plant closures. To encourage work sharing in lieu of layoffs, a few states have begun offering prorated unemployment benefits for workers whose hours are reduced because of slack work. With the onset of the recession in 1990, job security again moved to the forefront of labor market concerns in the United States.

Certainly layoffs, often on a large scale, are unavoidable in any competitive economy. But are jobs unnecessarily unstable in the United States? Could workers be offered more secure employment without placing excessive burdens on the companies that employ them? In fact U.S. employers are atypical in the extent to which they use layoffs to shed excess labor. Companies in many other industrialized countries rely far more heavily on alternatives to layoff, including work-sharing arrangements, attrition, hiring freezes, and early retirement.

In this book, we compare labor adjustment practices in the United States with those in the former West Germany.[2] A detailed examination

1. Vroman and Wissoker (1990, p. 35)
2. Although we refer to "Germany" at many points in the subsequent discussion, our analysis covers only the former West Germany.

of how the labor market operates in another country can improve our understanding of the U.S. labor market and stimulate our thinking about labor market policy.

The German experience is of interest for at least two reasons. First, German workers, on average, enjoy much greater job security than do U.S. workers. Historically, German workers have had considerable legal protection against layoffs, such as the right to advance notice of dismissal and the right to compensation in a mass layoff. While Germany's employment protection laws have received much attention in this country, other features of its labor market policies, such as the availability of partial unemployment insurance benefits for workers on reduced schedules and an extensive system of worker training, also help to bolster employment security.

Second, although Germany did experience high unemployment in the 1980s, its economy generally has been strong during the postwar period. Thus, on the surface German labor market policies seem compatible with a dynamic and competitive economy, although we will examine arguments to the contrary.

In this book, we address several questions. How do labor adjustment practices differ between Germany and the United States? How responsible are labor market policies and institutions for observed cross-country differences in adjustment practices? Does job security for workers inhibit necessary adjustment? What effects do labor adjustment practices have on who bears the burden of adjustment to economic shocks in the two countries? Finally, can the policies that help Germany increase the employment stability of workers be successfully transferred to the United States without burdening employers?

Proponents of greater job security have pointed to numerous benefits of policies that would reduce layoffs and encourage greater use of alternatives. When companies lay off workers in response to a temporary downturn in demand, they incur substantial costs associated with recalling those workers or hiring and training new workers when conditions improve. Permanently laid-off workers may experience extended periods of joblessness that could have been avoided had companies used attrition to achieve the same work force reductions. If, as we will argue, many layoffs occur because current U.S. policies bias employer decisions in favor of their use, the social costs associated with prevailing adjustment practices are inefficiently large.[3]

---

3. For an expanded discussion of efficiency arguments concerning job security regulation, see Houseman (1990).

Excessive layoffs also strain social services, most notably the health care system. Laid-off workers often lose their health insurance coverage, which means that laid-off workers and their families may become a drain on the medicaid system or on the private health care sector as nonpaying patients.

Moreover, there is a compelling equity argument for reducing layoffs. Compared with alternatives such as work sharing, extensive reliance on layoffs during a downturn concentrates the costs of adjustment on a relatively small number of workers. Laid-off workers often suffer large losses in income and other job-related benefits.

Opponents of policies to promote greater job security for workers argue that government intervention will generate costs that far outweigh any benefits. Measures to reduce layoffs, it is feared, will inhibit necessary labor adjustment, increase labor costs to companies, and lead to higher unemployment. Indeed, these views have been expressed in Germany and other European countries where employment protection laws such as those requiring advance notice of layoffs and compensation to laid-off workers have been blamed for the rise in unemployment during the 1980s. Echoing this sentiment, President Ronald Reagan described the advance notice bill passed by Congress in 1988 as "an apparent attempt to import Euro-malaise."[4]

The debate over such employment protection laws in the United States and in Europe, however, has generated more heat than light. While policymakers have been quick to condemn or condone these laws, little empirical support exists for either side's position. One purpose of this book is to provide a careful empirical examination of this issue.

In analyzing labor adjustment in Germany, we emphasize that one should not study employment protection laws in isolation, but rather as part of a larger set of labor market policies. The interactions among various policies are important for the way they affect labor adjustment. On the one hand, Germany's employment protection laws do raise the costs to employers of laying off workers. On the other hand, other policies compensate by subsidizing the cost of alternatives. For example, the German unemployment insurance system offers prorated benefits to workers whose hours have been cut back because of slack work. Since the unemployment insurance system in Germany is not experience rated, in contrast to the situation in the United States, employers that place workers on short time do not incur a tax penalty. These policies make short-time work a more acceptable alternative to layoffs for workers and

4. Langley and Seib (1988).

employers. The German government also has helped to subsidize the costs to companies of early retirement programs. During the 1970s and 1980s early retirement became a popular mechanism for reducing the work force while avoiding layoffs.

In a less direct though important way, Germany's extensive system of worker training, particularly its apprenticeship system, helps to reduce the costs to employers of providing job security. During a downturn an employer may avoid laying off excess workers by transferring them into positions vacated by workers who are retiring or quitting. In Germany this process of internal transfers is facilitated by the existence of a broadly-skilled work force, for which the country's apprenticeship system is widely credited.

Based on a statistical analysis of labor adjustment in manufacturing industries in Germany and the United States, we find little evidence to suggest that, taken together, German labor market policies inhibit adjustment. In the short run German employers adjust employment levels proportionately less to changes in demand than do their U.S. counterparts. However, in most industries employers fully compensate for this lack of short-run employment adjustment by making larger adjustments to average hours per worker. Thus, even in the short run the adjustment of total labor input is generally similar in the two countries. Fluctuations in short-time work account for a large fraction of short-run labor adjustment in German manufacturing, while temporary layoffs account for a large fraction of short-run adjustment in U.S. manufacturing. Over time horizons of a year to a year and a half, we generally find no significant difference in the adjustment of employment to demand changes in the two countries.

Overall, we conclude that German policies have been fairly successful at giving workers more stable employment without inhibiting labor adjustment and without imposing burdensome costs on employers. The success of German policies in Germany, however, does not necessarily mean they should be adopted wholesale in this country. Institutions differ, and policies that work well in one country may not be easily transferred to another. The policies that we recommend for the United States draw selectively from Germany's experience and build on the institutional structure in this country.

Rather than promoting job security, current U.S. policies bias employer decisions in favor of layoffs. Under our unemployment insurance system, benefits are available for workers who are laid off, but not, in general, for workers whose hours have been cut back for economic reasons. It is interesting to note that work-sharing schemes used to be a much more popular mechanism for reducing labor input during downturns in the United States. Work-sharing schemes were used extensively during the Great Depression of the 1930s. Labor historians have attributed the decline in work sharing and the rise in layoffs as the predominant mechanism of labor adjustment in this country in part to the introduction of unemployment insurance. The availability of unemployment insurance made layoffs more socially acceptable.[5] The German unemployment insurance system did not introduce this same bias against work sharing in favor of layoffs, for prorated unemployment insurance benefits for workers on short time have always been available.

The way in which unemployment insurance benefits are financed further encourages the use of layoffs. The unemployment insurance system in the United States is supported by revenues from a payroll tax. An individual employer's tax is based, in part, on that employer's history of layoffs. The experience rating of unemployment insurance taxes is imperfect, however, in the sense that the added taxes an employer pays as a result of laying off another worker are typically less than the costs to the unemployment insurance system of paying that worker benefits. Many policymakers and scholars have noted that, because of the imperfect experience rating of unemployment insurance taxes, employers lay off too many workers.

Furthermore, if laid-off workers or uninsured members of their families require medical attention, they are likely to become medicaid patients or nonpaying private sector patients. The fact that these individuals' health care costs are at least partially absorbed by a third party encourages excessive reliance on layoffs.

To help correct the pro-layoff bias of current policy, we recommend adoption of a series of measures at the federal and state level. In recent years fourteen states have experimented with providing prorated unemployment benefits to workers on short time. One of our recommendations is that short-time compensation (STC) programs be introduced in the remaining states. We also recommend that measures be taken to increase the use of STC programs in states that already have such programs. For example, in a number of states with STC programs,

---

5. For discussions of the importance of work sharing historically in the United States see Jacoby (1985) and Carter and Sutch (1991). Jacoby also discusses the role that unemployment insurance played in the decline of work sharing during the 1940s and 1950s.

employers who put workers on short time may incur much higher unemployment insurance taxes than if they simply lay workers off. We recommend that these differences in the tax treatment of layoffs and short time be eliminated. Administrative rules associated with state STC programs, such as reporting requirements and restrictions on work schedules, may also inhibit the use of work-sharing schemes. Paperwork should be reduced and programs should be modified to allow employers more flexibility in the scheduling of workers on short time.

The cost of maintaining fringe benefits is another deterrent to using short time.[6] While layoffs allow employers to reduce their fringe benefit costs, the loss of benefits, especially health insurance, imposes substantial costs on both laid-off workers and the public purse. The existence of a large population without health insurance coverage has become a major policy concern in this country. We recommend that state governments provide subsidies or loans to help cover the cost to companies of maintaining certain benefits for workers on short time. The cost of this program would be offset, at least in part, by lower expenditures on medicaid.

To take advantage of STC programs, employers must be aware of their availability. Yet, a recent survey of employers in three states with STC programs found that half of the employers who were not using the programs did not know they existed.[7] Greater publicity for STC programs is a simple and relatively low cost measure but is nevertheless essential for the program's success.

In addition to introducing and strengthening STC programs to encourage greater work sharing during downturns, we recommend several measures to discourage excessive layoffs and assist dislocated workers. First, the experience rating of the unemployment insurance system should be increased. Unemployment insurance taxes paid by an employer are determined by that employer's tax rate applied to the wages paid each worker up to a certain ceiling, which varies from state to state. In all states an employer's tax rate depends to some degree on its layoff history; however, states set minimum and maximum tax rates. Employers who are already at the maximum rate face no penalty for laying

6. Although state laws typically do not require companies to maintain the fringe benefits of workers on short time, most companies do so. An employer that temporarily cuts benefits for workers on short time is likely to encounter personnel and administrative problems.

7. See Kerachsky and others (1985, p. 163).

off additional workers. In this situation the experience-rating principle most seriously breaks down. In recent years, the federal and state governments have addressed this problem by increasing the maximum tax rate. We recommend further tightening of the experience rating of unemployment insurance taxes.

Although since 1989 U.S. employers have been required to provide notice of mass layoffs, the U.S. law is weak by international standards. Under certain circumstances, a company may still lay off hundreds of workers without being obliged to notify in advance those affected. We recommend strengthening notice requirements.[8]

In many countries, including Germany, a large share of laid-off workers receive legally mandated severance payments. While we do not recommend that U.S. companies be required to make severance payments to workers they lay off, we do recommend they be required to continue the health insurance coverage of laid-off workers for one to two months. This requirement would reduce the hardship faced by these workers while alleviating some of the social costs of layoffs.

Finally, following a 1990 report by the Office of Technology Assessment for Congress, we point to the benefits of adopting certain policies patterned on the German apprenticeship training model. According to one estimate, German companies spend roughly twice as much per worker on training as do U.S. companies.[9] Most of the difference is accounted for by the low investments U.S. companies make in apprenticeship training compared with German companies. One deterrent to investment in training in the United States is the fear that employees in whom a company makes substantial training investments will leave to work for competitors. Because companies cannot be assured that they will reap all of the benefits from their investments, they may invest less heavily than is socially optimal. There also are likely to be economies of scale associated with many types of worker training such that small companies do not find it in their interest to make these investments.

In Germany two factors mitigate these problems. Not only does the government help pay for the costs of apprenticeship training, but also in many instances companies share training costs through employers' associations. One policy option for the United States would be to support the formation of industry consortia that could pool the costs and

8. We review evidence on the benefits and costs of notice requirements in chap. 6.
9. Cited in Hilton (1991, p. 33).

benefits of training across affiliated companies. Currently, the Department of Labor provides limited funding for such activities through demonstration projects.

The most tangible benefit from increased worker training is higher productivity. But worker training also increases employment security. As already mentioned, companies can avoid laying off excess workers by transferring them into jobs vacated by workers who quit or retire. Such transfers are less costly if workers possess a broad set of skills. Moreover, in the event of a layoff, a worker with a good set of skills should find reemployment easier.

Overview of the Book

The focus of our book is the examination of how labor market institutions affect the way in which companies adjust labor to changing demand conditions. Labor adjustment practices, in turn, have important implications for workers' employment security and for the distribution of the costs of adjustment across workers. Chapter 2 provides background on labor market policies and other aspects of the industrial relations systems in Germany and the United States. We point out that mutually reinforcing policies in Germany encourage employers to use work sharing and other alternatives to layoffs. In contrast, in the United States public policies encourage the use of layoffs rather than alternatives.

Chapter 3 presents an overview of the German and U.S. macroeconomies during the 1970s and 1980s, focusing on trends in unemployment. A common perception is that Germany and other European countries experienced much higher unemployment rates than the United States in the 1980s and that the presence of stringent employment protection laws was partially responsible for this difference. However, if one looks at unemployment numbers adjusted for differences in the definition of unemployment across countries, Germany's unemployment rate was the same as or lower than the U.S. rate throughout the period. Nevertheless, Germany did experience tremendous growth in unemployment from the mid-1970s through the mid-1980s, and we review various explanations for that increase. No empirical evidence supports the hypothesis that German labor market policies were responsible for the growth in unemployment during that period. Academic economists have tended to support other theories.

Chapter 4 presents our own evidence related to this issue. Using carefully matched German and U.S. data for manufacturing industries, we examine the adjustment of employment and hours worked to demand shocks in the two countries. We find that although over a short time the adjustment of employment levels is significantly greater in the United States for most industries, the adjustment of total hours is not, implying that German employers compensate for the lack of employment adjustment by adjusting average hours per worker more than do U.S. employers. Over a year to a year and a half, there is no consistent difference in the adjustment of employment levels to changes in demand in the two countries. We also highlight the importance of short-time work in German manufacturing by showing that short-time work accounts for a large percentage of the fluctuations in total hours in that sector. Temporary layoffs followed by recalls account for a smaller but still substantial percentage of the fluctuations in employment levels in U.S. manufacturing industries. By implication, the introduction of STC programs, which primarily are intended to avert temporary layoffs, could greatly reduce employment fluctuations in the United States.

In chapter 5 we explore some of the distributional effects of the prevailing labor adjustment practices in the two countries. The extensive use of layoffs during downturns in the United States concentrates the burden of adjustment on a relatively small number of workers, while the greater use of average hours adjustment in Germany helps spread the adjustment across a larger number of workers. Although U.S. workers, on average, have less job security than German workers, certain groups of workers in the United States enjoy substantial job protection. It is well known that blue-collar work in the United States is characterized by considerable employment instability. We show that, at least until recently, white-collar workers have enjoyed much greater job security and examine various explanations for the difference in treatment of blue-collar and white-collar workers. In addition, because of the prevalence of seniority-based layoffs, youth and to some extent women bear a disproportionate amount of adjustment to economic changes.

In Germany, although workers receive relatively strong employment protection, German policies protect certain groups of workers better than others. The employment of women is somewhat more volatile than that of men. German immigration policies and, in recent years, early retirement programs have also shifted some of the adjustment onto foreign workers and older workers.

In chapter 6 we review trends in U.S. policy and recommend further changes. We argue that in small though important ways recent private and public sector initiatives have increased employment security in the United States and moved us somewhat closer to the German model. Our recommendations build on these recent trends.

CHAPTER TWO

Industrial Relations

THE INDUSTRIAL RELATIONS systems in Germany and the United States differ in many respects. We are especially interested in how institutional differences help to explain the differences in labor adjustment practices in the two countries. We focus on selected aspects of each country's industrial relations: worker representation, plant closing and mass layoff laws, unemployment insurance, and vocational education and training. Besides drawing comparisons between specific German and U.S. policies, we emphasize the interrelationships among policies within each country. For example, though dismissal laws may make it more costly for German companies to lay off workers, unemployment insurance for short-time work and government-subsidized early retirement schemes, among other policies, make it less expensive for German companies to offer strong job security.

The institutional differences in the two countries lead us to expect different patterns of labor adjustment in response to changing demand conditions. We would expect American employers to rely relatively more heavily on adjustment of employment levels, and German employers to rely relatively more heavily on adjustment of average hours per worker, at least in the short run. We would also expect institutional differences to have important implications for how the costs of adjustment are distributed across groups of workers in the two countries. These issues are addressed empirically in chapters 4 and 5.

Industrial Relations in Germany

We begin our discussion of industrial relations in Germany with an overview of its system of worker representation. This background is important for understanding labor's influence on adjustment practices. Next, we turn to various public policies that affect labor adjustment practices in Germany. Best known are Germany's employment protection laws, which stipulate restrictions on companies' use of layoffs. We also discuss the German short-time unemployment insurance system and government-subsidized early retirement programs, which promote the use of alternatives to layoffs. Finally, we briefly discuss the German apprenticeship system and consider the argument that this system of vocational training has made the German work force highly skilled and flexible and thereby has facilitated the use of alternatives to layoffs.

Worker Representation in Germany: Unions and Codetermination

Workers in Germany have two channels of representation: privately organized trade unions and the government-mandated system of code-termination. Trade unions in Germany are highly centralized, with a primary federation consisting of sixteen industrial unions. Unions and employers' associations negotiate collective agreements that cover wages and also sometimes certain benefits at the regional or national level. Single-employer contracts, such as that between the metal workers' union and Volkswagen, account for only a very small share of all workers covered by collective bargaining agreements.[1]

The system of codetermination provides for employee representation in the workplace and has two components. At establishments with five or more employees, workers have the legal right to form a works council. This body of worker representatives has codetermination powers in such areas as scheduling, workplace safety, and hiring and firing. The works council plays an important role in negotiating settlements in the event of mass layoffs or plant closures. In large companies, workers also elect representatives to the company's supervisory board, which has responsibilities similar to those of the board of directors at a U.S. firm.

In theory, trade unions, works councils, and worker representatives on the supervisory board have clearly delineated jurisdictions: trade unions engage in collective bargaining at the regional or national level; works councils are concerned with local personnel policy; and worker

---

1. Brandes, Meyer, and Schudlich (1991, p. 41) report that, in 1990, about 2,000 enterprises negotiated individual contracts with a union. These single-employer agreements accounted for only about 6 percent of all workers covered by collective bargaining agreements.

representatives on the supervisory board deal with broad company policy. In practice, however, the distinctions among these three bodies are less clear-cut. Works councilors typically are union members and unions usually play an important supportive role for the works councils. Similarly, many worker representatives on supervisory boards are also works councilors and union members.[2]

Unions

The German labor movement dates back to the mid-nineteenth century. Collective bargaining took hold as the principal mechanism for regulating the workplace following World War I under the Weimar Republic. However, unions and the system of collective bargaining came under attack during the depression in the 1930s, and trade unions were formally banned by the Nazi government.

During the occupation of Germany following World War II, the Allied Forces revamped German labor law and industrial relations. Unions were reorganized and unified into industrial unions that encompass all political and ideological wings. The establishment of a unified, highly centralized union organization was seen as a counterweight to strong German business.

The principal trade union organization is the German Trade Union Federation (Deutscher Gewerkschaftsbund, or DGB). The DGB comprises sixteen industrial unions that represent blue- and white-collar workers and cover workers in all sectors of the economy, including the public sector. DGB unions face only limited competition from non-affiliated unions. The German Staff Union (Deutsche Angestellten-Gewerkschaft, or DAG) represents some white-collar workers, the German Association of Civil Servants (Deutscher Beamtenbund, DBB) represents tenured civil servants, and a small number of workers belong to the German Christian Union (Christlicher Gewerkschaftsbund Deutschland, CGD). As of the mid-1980s, more than 80 percent of all German union members belonged to DGB unions.[3] About 40 percent of wage and salary earners are union members. Thus, union membership is far higher in Germany than in the United States, where just over 15 percent

2. For general discussions of collective bargaining in Germany, see Flanagan, Soskice, and Ulman (1983, pp. 222–75); Brandes, Meyer, and Schudlich (1991); and Pacqué (undated). Federal Minister of Labor and Social Affairs (1980) provides an overview of the German system of codetermination.

3. Statistisches Bundesamt (1987, p. 600).

of wage and salary workers belonged to unions in the mid-1980s. In contrast to trends in the United States, union density in Germany has risen modestly over the last two decades.[4]

Employers' Associations

The evolution of German employers' associations parallels that of trade unions. Employers' associations were first formed in Germany in the nineteenth century in response to the strengthening of labor unions, and by the turn of the century were quite well developed. Although the central role of employers' associations became collective bargaining in the 1930s, their original purpose was not to negotiate with the unions but rather to counter union influence in the work force. Like the labor unions, the employers' associations were banned by the Nazi government and were reinstituted following World War II.

About 80 percent of all firms employing about 90 percent of all workers in the private sector belong to employers' associations. Thus, the organization rate among employers is considerably higher than that among employees. The umbrella organization, the Federal Union of German Employers' Associations (Bundesvereinigung der deutschen Arbeitgeberverbände, BdA) comprises several hundred regional and about fifty national employers' associations.[5]

Given this high degree of organization, it has been argued that the employers' associations are much stronger than the trade unions. Employers' associations have been able to maintain discipline among their members. For example, they have been successful in getting employers to participate in lockouts, in part because they have the financial resources needed to back companies taking industrial action.

Collective Bargaining

Collective agreements for broad industrial sectors are negotiated by unions and employers' associations at the regional or national level. Even when bargaining occurs at the regional level, however, the provisions negotiated tend to be similar across regions within an industry. The issues subject to collective bargaining are circumscribed by the highly centralized character of the negotiations and by the existence of works

4. Freeman (1989, p. 130).
5. Brandes, Meyer, and Schudlich (1991, pp. 39, 41).

councils with jurisdiction over personnel policy. Unions and employers' associations negotiate primarily over wages and some benefits. In the 1980s shorter working hours also became a major collective bargaining issue.

It should be emphasized that negotiated wage levels only set the minimum amounts that an employer must pay. An employer can always choose to offer workers a higher wage scale. Although a union that has negotiated an industry-level agreement is legally prohibited from further negotiations with individual employers, collective agreements may stipulate that the works council can bargain with the individual employer further over wages and benefits. Thus, although negotiation over wage levels is primarily within the unions' jurisdiction, works councils often engage in a second level of negotiations over compensation with individual employers.

The collective agreement is only binding for companies that are members of the signatory employers' association. However, even non-members generally choose to comply with its terms. And the collective agreement may be formally extended to the entire industry by the federal or state labor minister. For such an extension to occur, at least 50 percent of all employees in the industrial sector must work for firms represented by the employers' association, the extension must be approved by the union and the employers' association, and the federal or state labor minister must determine that it serves the public interest.

Working days lost owing to industrial strife are low in Germany even when compared with the United States, where the percentage of the work force represented by a union is much lower.[6] Major strikes are infrequent and usually have been initiated by the metal workers' union or the printers' union. One reason for the relatively peaceful industrial climate is that German law strictly limits the use of strikes. Strikes are generally prohibited except in the event of a failure of negotiations over a new collective agreement and must be preceded by a secret ballot of union members. Works councils, which oversee the administration of collective agreements, are prohibited from calling a strike. Some observers have argued that these limitations on strikes seriously weaken labor's bargaining power.[7] Employers' associations have effectively countered strikes with lockouts when they have occurred.

6. Figures reported by the International Labour Organization (1990) indicate that only 0.002 percent of total work time was lost because of strikes in Germany during 1989, compared with 0.070 percent in the United States in the same year.

7. Flanagan, Soskice, and Ulman (1983, p. 236).

A law passed in 1986 further limits the usefulness of the strike weapon to unions. To save their strike funds, unions had selectively struck establishments that were key suppliers of other companies, forcing these companies to shut as well. Workers laid off from companies whose supplies were cut because of a strike could collect unemployment insurance benefits under previous German law. The new law stipulates that workers who are laid off by companies owing to lack of work during a strike are ineligible for unemployment insurance benefits if they also would benefit from the strike demands being met.

Works Councils

The dual system of worker representation in unions and in works councils dates back to the nineteenth century in Germany. Initially works councils were established by employers to keep unions out of their plants and to legitimize employers' policies for the plants. A law enacted in 1920 required companies to establish works councils. Although unions had begun to support representation in the plants, they opposed the 1920 law because works councils were formally separate from the unions and they feared the councils would become a tool of management. The Nazi government abolished the works councils, just as they did the unions and employers' associations.

The Works Constitution Act of 1952 reestablished the right of workers to an elected works council. An amendment to this act passed in 1972 greatly strengthened the role of works councils in staffing and personnel policy. The law gives workers in every establishment with five or more workers the right to form a works council. Multiplant operations have a separate works council for each plant along with a central works council. The law also provides for the establishment of a committee for economic affairs at enterprises with more than one hundred employees.

If workers fail to establish a works council, however, they lose all rights given to the works council. According to one estimate, only about 20 percent of all establishments covered by the law have a works council. Establishments without works councils, however, tend to be small. Virtually all establishments with six hundred or more employees have works councils. As a consequence, in spite of the small share of establishments with works councils, about 65 percent of private sector wage and salary earners are represented by works councils.[8]

8. Sengenberger (1985, p. 7).

Works councils have the right to information, consultation, and codecision with management in a wide range of matters concerning personnel policy. Works councils must approve the use of overtime and short-time work and the structure of the day (for instance, standard shift hours and the spacing of breaks). The works council must be consulted before the hiring, firing, and dismissal of any worker, though management retains the final say in these matters. The works council also has substantive powers in the event of a mass layoff. Besides informing and consulting the works council, management must negotiate a social plan with the works council that provides compensation to laid-off workers.

Worker Representation on the Supervisory Board

The supervisory board of German companies selects the company's management and has some control over the company's activities. The Codetermination Act for Coal Mining, Iron, and Steel of 1951 stipulates the election of worker representatives to the supervisory boards of companies with 1,000 or more employees in these industries. In these companies workers and shareholders have an equal number of representatives on the supervisory board. The chair is a neutral third party who must be approved by worker and shareholder representatives. A weakened version of codetermination was extended to all companies with 500 or more employees in the Works Constitution Act of 1952. Under this law worker representatives compose one-third of the supervisory board.

In 1976 codetermination was strengthened in companies with 2,000 or more employees. In these companies workers and shareholders have equal representation on the supervisory board, as in companies with 1,000 or more employees in the coal mining and iron and steel industries. The chair is elected by a majority and in a deadlock, the chair is elected by the shareholders' representatives. Therefore, in contrast to the situation in large coal mining and iron and steel companies, the shareholders retain majority control of the supervisory board in other large companies.

Employment Protection Laws

German law strictly regulates the conditions under which workers may be dismissed from their jobs. In contrast to the situation in the

United States, in Germany there is no such thing as a temporary layoff. German workers who are dismissed have no recall rights, and they lose their entitlement to most company benefits (pensions are the principal exception). The term dismissal covers both dismissals for individual conduct and layoffs for economic reasons. All dismissals in Germany must be socially justified. When a dismissal is legal, certain procedures must be followed. In an individual dismissal, the employer must give the worker advance notice of the dismissal. In a collective dismissal, the local labor office and the works council have some power to affect the timing and the terms of the layoff.[9]

Laws regulating dismissals have deep historical roots in Germany.[10] Laws requiring employers to justify dismissals date back to 1920. Laws requiring advance notice of dismissal were first passed in 1926. Under current law, a dismissal may be justified for reasons having to do with the individual (for example, because of the individual's behavior or poor performance) or for economic reasons. Dismissals for economic reasons are justified only if the affected individuals cannot be reasonably trans- ferred elsewhere in the company and the company has exhausted all other means of avoiding layoffs, such as the reduction of overtime and the introduction of short-time work. In the case of dismissal for eco- nomic reasons, the law also sets out broad criteria to be used in selecting individuals for layoffs. In particular, the law requires that age, marital status, whether a person has dependents, and other factors affecting the hardship a layoff would cause for the individual and his or her family be considered. Therefore, the process of selecting individuals for layoff is more complex than in the United States where seniority is the dom- inant criterion used.

Works councils must be consulted before every dismissal. The works council may oppose the dismissal on certain grounds, although it cannot prevent the employer from dismissing a worker. However, the dismissed worker may bring his or her case before the labor court, and he or she

9. Legal requirements concerning dismissals may be strengthened through the collective bargaining process. Warnken and Ronning (1990, pp. 239–42) report that contract provisions restricting dismissals in situations involving the introduction of new technology or other rationalizations of the work process and protecting workers with long tenures from ordinary dismissals had become relatively common by the mid-1980s.

10. This is also true in many European countries. For discussions of the history of employment protection laws in other countries, see Meyers (1964) and Houseman (1990). For a discussion of the development of these laws in Germany, see Weiss (1987).

is more likely to be awarded reinstatement or compensation if the works council has opposed the dismissal.

If the dismissal is deemed socially justified, the employer must notify the individual before dismissal. Required periods of notice to individual workers vary from two weeks to six months, depending on whether the worker holds a blue-collar or a white-collar job and on his or her seniority and age. For example, a blue-collar worker with less than five years of seniority is entitled to only two weeks of notice, one with ten to twenty years of seniority is entitled to two to three months of notice, and one with more than twenty years of seniority is entitled to three to six months of notice. White-collar workers are entitled to somewhat longer notice than are blue-collar workers with comparable seniority. Notice for white-collar workers ranges from six weeks for those with less than five years of service to three to six months for those with more than twelve years of service. [11]

German law requires that employers follow additional procedures in a collective dismissal. The definition of a collective dismissal varies by size of establishment. The thresholds that must be crossed before a reduction in force constitutes a collective dismissal are not particularly high. For example, until 1985, a dismissal of 10 percent or more of the work force within a thirty-day period in establishments with 60 to 250 workers constituted a collective dismissal. In establishments with 500 or more workers, the dismissal of just 30 workers over a thirty-day period was legally classified as a collective dismissal. As indicated in table 2-1, these thresholds have been raised somewhat since 1985.

The Protection against Dismissal Act of 1951 and the Works Constitution Act of 1952 established notification and consultation requirements for employers prior to collective dismissals. The 1951 act requires employers to notify and consult with the works council and to notify the state employment office thirty days before carrying out a collective dismissal. The state government may delay the layoff for up to two months, but it cannot prevent it. The 1952 act requires employers to consult the works council "as soon as possible" when contemplating a

11. A 1990 decision of the Federal Constitutional Court (Bundesverfassungsgericht), the highest German court, declared the disparate treatment of blue-collar and white-collar workers under these statutes to be unconstitutional. This decision instructed the parliament to pass new legislation providing for equal notice periods for the two groups prior to June 30, 1993. The most likely outcome is that notice periods for blue-collar workers will be lengthened to correspond to those provided for white-collar workers (Brandes, Meyer, and Schudlich, 1992, pp. 22–23).

Table 2-1. *Definition of a Collective Dismissal in Germany before and after 1985*

Number of employees in the establishment	Minimum number of dismissals over a thirty-day period	
	Pre-1985	Post-1985
20–59	6	20% of employees and at least 6 workers
60–250	10% of employees	20% of employees and at least 37 workers
251–499	26	15% of employees and at least 60 workers
500 and more	30	10% of employees and at least 60 workers

dismissal and to discuss alternatives to layoffs with the works council before dismissing anyone. However, if no compromise is reached between management and the works council, management retains all decisionmaking authority.

Legislation passed in 1969 strengthened the notice requirement by stipulating that employers should keep the works council and the local employment office advised of any developments that might lead to layoffs over the next twelve months; by requiring that, in a layoff, the local employment office should determine whether the employer had provided due notice; and by permitting the government to collect compensation from the employer for up to six months of expenditures for retraining dismissed employees if the government determines that the notice given was inadequate.

A more fundamental change was introduced with the amendment of the Works Constitution Act in 1972. This law took effect in 1973 and provides that in a collective dismissal at an establishment normally employing more than twenty employees, management and the works council must negotiate a social plan that specifies compensation for laid-off workers. The social plan may specify not only financial compensation, but also retraining benefits or the transfer of workers to other parts of the enterprise. If the two parties cannot agree on the provisions of the social plan, the law provides for binding arbitration.

In addition, the 1972 act requires that management provide the works council with full and timely information concerning their plans for a plant closure or mass dismissal and any alternatives that it is considering. Management must also try to reach a "compromise of interest" with the works council over the closure or mass dismissal. The intention of this provision of the act is to give the works council the information it needs to participate in the decisionmaking process in a meaningful way.

Although Germany's various employment protection laws on the surface seem to significantly constrain employer behavior, some observers have argued that many of the provisions in these laws have had little practical effect on business decisions to close plants and lay off workers. For example, even though management is legally required to provide the works council with full information about plans for a collective dismissal, Manfred Weiss asserts that such information is typically hidden for as long as possible.[12] The company can be fined 20,000 deutsche marks (DM) for breaking the law, but Weiss argues that this sanction has been ineffective because it must be proven in court that the company concealed information deliberately and because companies view the amount of the potential fine as low relative to the economic costs of early disclosure of a partial or total shutdown.

Similarly, Weiss argues that, because companies fear disclosure of confidential information, the law requiring management to inform the state labor office and the works council of all measures to be taken in the next twelve months that could lead to dismissals is rarely obeyed. Employers who can be proven to have willfully violated the law or to have violated it by gross negligence are subject to sanction, but, according to Weiss, the courts have raised the standard of proof on these issues so much that the law is virtually unenforceable.

The requirement that employers negotiate a social plan before a collective dismissal is widely regarded as the most important provision in collective dismissal law. Compensation under a social plan varies greatly according to the worker's tenure and salary. Compensation also depends on the financial condition of the firm. Settlements in social plans tend to be far lower in bankruptcy cases than in other cases.

A recent survey of social plans conducted by the Institute of German Industry (Institut der deutschen Wirtschaft), the research arm of the BdA, documents substantial variability in awards.[13] In a sample of 145 social plans negotiated between 1980 and 1985, the median per worker settlement was about 11,000 DM. Weekly earnings of blue-collar workers in the industrial sector averaged just under 650 DM per week in 1984, so the median settlement represented about seventeen weeks'

12. Weiss (1986, pp. 32, 38).
13. For a summary of the results of the survey, see Hemmer (1988).

earnings.[14] However, about 17 percent of those laid off received under 5,000 DM and 26 percent received over 20,000 DM.

Throughout the 1970s and 1980s German unemployment rose steadily. Many blamed this development, in part, on the regulation of dismissals, which had become more stringent since the early 1970s. Employers allegedly hesitated to hire new workers because of the high costs of dismissing them should their performance be poor or should economic conditions worsen.

The 1985 Employment Promotion Act was designed to ease restrictions on dismissals by increasing the number of exemptions from the law. Before 1985, employers had to negotiate a social plan if they dismissed about 10 percent or more of their work force within a thirty-day period; the threshold was even lower for large firms. The 1985 act raised that minimum to about 20 percent of the work force over a thirty-day period for small establishments, to about 15 percent for medium-sized establishments, and to 10 percent for large establishments (see table 2-1). In addition, new enterprises are exempted from any requirement to negotiate a social plan for four years.

Although these higher thresholds will tend to reduce the number of instances where social plans must be negotiated, the net effect of the law could be to increase the number of social plans. Before 1985, employers frequently tried to avoid triggering social plan requirements by negotiating voluntary severance payment contracts with individuals. Under the 1985 law, terminations by mutual agreement that are initiated by management count as work force reductions in determining whether a social plan must be negotiated.[15]

The 1985 Employment Promotion Act also relaxed restrictions on the use of temporary workers and fixed-term contracts. Germany's dismissal laws do not apply to individuals on fixed-term contracts or to workers supplied by a temporary help agency. So that employers cannot circumvent these laws by employing workers on temporary status, the use of such workers is strictly limited. The 1985 act, however, extended the permissible length of a fixed-term contract from six months to eighteen months for an ongoing enterprise and to twenty-four months

14. Statistisches Bundesamt (1987, p. 484).
15. See Weiss (1986, p. 41). The negotiation of voluntary severance payment contracts is still quite popular. By using these contracts employers avoid having to consult the works council on each dismissal. Moreover, they minimize employee morale problems associated with layoffs and help preserve the company's reputation as a good employer.

for a small new business.[16] The law also extended the period that an agency temporary can work for a particular company from three months to six months.

The use of fixed-term contracts has grown dramatically since the passage of the 1985 Employment Promotion Act. From 1984 to 1988 the number of workers on fixed-term contracts grew by 46 percent and accounted for 44 percent of the increase in wage and salary employment in Germany.[17] However, no consensus has emerged on the causes of these recent changes. Christoph F. Büchtemann has argued that much of the increase was unrelated to the new regulations.[18] German employers interviewed for this study also downplayed the importance of this change in the law.

Government Programs to Promote Alternatives to Layoffs

While employment protection laws discourage layoffs in Germany, various government programs subsidize the use of alternatives to layoffs and thereby ease the costs to German employers of providing job security for their work force. Two of the most important program areas have been unemployment insurance for short-time work and subsidized early retirement.

THE UNEMPLOYMENT INSURANCE SYSTEM AND SHORT-TIME WORK. An important feature of the German unemployment insurance system is the provision for short-time benefits, which was first established in 1927.[19] With the approval of the Federal Employment Service (Bundesanstalt für Arbeit) and the company's works council, employees whose hours of work have been reduced can collect prorated unemployment insurance benefits. For example, an employee who works four days a week instead of five would receive 80 percent of his or her pay plus 20 percent of the unemployment insurance benefits to which he or she

16. Fixed-term contracts of longer than six months' duration have always been allowed under certain circumstances, including the replacement of absent permanent employees and the carrying out of special tasks that are temporary in nature. The courts had ruled, however, that uncertainty about future labor demand was not a legitimate reason for use of extended fixed-term contracts. The new law allows longer fixed-term contracts without requiring the employer to give a reason for their use. See Büchtemann (1989).

17. Büchtemann (1989, p. 8).

18. Büchtemann (1989, 1990).

19. Flechsenhar (1980) provides a comprehensive discussion of short-time benefits in Germany. See also Meisel (1984, pp. 56–57); and Grais (1983, pp. 88–92).

would be entitled if wholly unemployed. This amounts to roughly 68 percent of previous net pay or, since 1984, 63 percent for workers without children; these replacement rates are much higher than those in the United States.[20]

The administration of the German short-time program is quite flexible. An employer operating under an approved short-time plan may further reduce working time without government approval if product demand is weaker than had been anticipated, provided that the works council agrees to the new plan. The employer can always unilaterally increase hours for workers on short time. After the workers are back on full time, the employer may reinstitute short time without government approval of a new plan for up to three months. There is also considerable flexibility in how hours reductions are achieved. Reductions in hours may vary considerably across workers. Those on short time may work fewer hours per day or fewer days each week, or they may be put on rotating layoffs.[21]

By law, employers placing workers on short time must maintain contributions to the national health insurance and pension funds at the same level as if the worker were fully employed, paying both the employer and the worker share of the applicable social insurance taxes on the difference between the worker's usual and short-time earnings. The Bundesanstalt für Arbeit reimburses the employer for the worker share of public pension fund contributions on this earnings shortfall.

In contrast to the situation in the United States, the unemployment insurance taxes German employers pay are not experience rated. That is, a German firm's unemployment insurance tax rate does not depend on the extent to which its employees collect unemployment insurance benefits or benefits for short-time work. Regulations governing dismissal arguably serve to inhibit employers from relying excessively on layoffs to reduce the work force. There are some significant restrictions on the use of short-time work as well. Short-time benefits are intended to be paid only to workers experiencing hours reductions as the result of temporary, but not seasonal, reductions in demand. In addition, companies applying for short-time benefits must show that other mea-

20. Although there is a cap on the benefit amount that is payable in Germany, this limit is quite high, and less than 1 percent of the unemployed are affected. See Hunt (1992, p. 5).

21. For a discussion of the administration of the German short-time system, see Vroman (1992).

sures for accommodating the fall in demand, such as reductions in overtime and the rebuilding of inventories, have already been taken. The reduction in hours the firm seeks to achieve also must attain certain proportions.

Interestingly, as the law pertaining to dismissals has been strengthened over time, the unemployment insurance system has been liberalized to permit more extensive use of short-time benefits. Indeed, the 1969 reform of the unemployment insurance system explicitly recognizes the preservation of employment relationships as the primary motivation for paying short-time benefits, stating that short-time allowances should be granted if doing so "will enable the employees concerned to keep their jobs and the establishment to keep experienced labor."

Before 1969, short-time benefits were payable only if a majority of the work force had their hours reduced by at least one-sixth for at least two weeks. Under current law, a third of the work force must have their hours reduced by at least one-tenth for at least four weeks. Although the period for which the hours reduction must last has been lengthened, the rules governing the use of short time have become more lenient about the size of the hours reduction at any point in time. Whereas before 1969 short time could not be used unless the firm desired at least an 8 percent reduction in total hours, today it can be used when the desired reduction in hours is as little as 3 percent.

The length of time that an establishment can make use of short-time benefits has also been extended. Before 1969, an establishment's work force could draw short-time benefits for no more than six months. As part of the 1969 reform of the unemployment insurance system, the law was changed so that establishments in depressed regions or depressed industries were permitted to use short-time benefits for up to twelve months. In 1975, the allowable period for having workers on short time was increased to twenty-four months during periods of general recession. Finally, a special provision introduced in 1983 allowed establishments in the steel industry to draw short-time benefits for as long as thirty-six months. These changes to the law have allowed companies to use short-time work schemes during recessions when the labor reduction is temporary and during restructuring when the downsizing required is more permanent. Companies engaged in long-term restructuring have been able to minimize layoffs by using short-time work schemes while their work force was being reduced through attrition and, in many cases, early retirement.

EARLY RETIREMENT. During the 1970s and 1980s German employers made extensive use of early retirement schemes to shed excess labor. As with short-time work, firms employing these schemes have received large public subsidies, a fact that undoubtedly has contributed to their popularity. Workers may retire early and receive a government pension under a variety of conditions. During the 1980s, when unemployment was rising sharply, the government established new early retirement programs or liberalized the use of existing ones.

One popular early retirement program allows workers, aged 60, who have contributed to the pension system for at least fifteen years and who have been unemployed for at least fifty-two weeks out of the last year and a half to start receiving a government pension. Companies tacitly used this provision to subsidize their own early retirement schemes by "firing" workers at age 59. These workers received unemployment insurance for a year, typically supplemented by payments from their companies, and then went on early retirement at age 60.

Beginning in the mid-1980s the government implicitly began to subsidize retirement at even earlier ages by changing the rules about unemployment insurance coverage for older workers. Germany has two separate benefit programs for unemployed workers. Unemployment insurance (Arbeitslosengeld) pays unemployed workers tax-free benefits at a rate sufficient to replace about 68 percent of previous net pay (or, since 1984, 63 percent for those with no dependent children). Unemployment insurance ordinarily can be collected for up to a year. The second, unemployment assistance (Arbeitslosenhilfe), is means tested and pays unemployed workers who qualify tax-free benefits at a rate sufficient to replace about 58 percent of previous net pay (or, since 1984, 56 percent for those with no dependent children). Unemployment assistance is most often drawn by unemployed workers who have exhausted their regular unemployment insurance benefits and in principle can be paid indefinitely, though individuals with substantial assets or other sources of family income cannot receive it.

The maximum period for which older, unemployed workers can receive unemployment insurance benefits—the higher, non-means-tested payments—has been extended several times. In 1985 the maximum period was lengthened from twelve to eighteen months for workers aged 49 and over. In 1986 the maximum period was set at sixteen months for workers aged 44 through 48, twenty months for workers aged 49 through 53, and twenty-four months for those aged 54 and over. And in 1987 the maximum period was set at eighteen months for workers aged 42 or 43, twenty-two months for those aged 44 through 48, twenty-six months for those aged 49 through 53, and thirty-two months for those aged 54 and over.[22] These extensions of the maximum period of receipt of unemployment insurance have had the effect of allowing government-subsidized early retirement at successively younger ages. Under the most recent law, a worker aged 57 years and four months can be dismissed and receive unemployment insurance, possibly supplemented by a company payment, for thirty-two months, and then begin collecting a government pension at age 60.

The government has tried to pass back some of the costs to certain companies that use the unemployment insurance scheme to finance early retirement measures. A law passed in 1982 requires companies to reimburse the government for the amount of unemployment insurance paid out to older workers they dismissed. However, the law exempts small firms, firms in economic trouble that need to substantially reduce their work force, and firms that otherwise are receiving public assistance. Many companies that were using the unemployment insurance system to finance early retirement measures, therefore, were covered by these exceptions.

Early retirement by unemployed workers under the provisions just described increased steadily in the mid-1970s and 1980s. Individuals in this scheme represented fewer than 2 percent of all new entrants into the pension system in 1974. Their numbers grew to account for 6 percent of all new pension recipients, and 11 percent of males entering the pension rolls, by 1984.[23]

The Preretirement Act of 1984, initially enacted for a four-year period and later extended, was a direct response to the high unemployment prevailing in Germany in the mid-1980s. The intention of the act was to open up jobs for the unemployed by subsidizing early retirement. Under the program, the participating company had to agree to pay the early retiree at least 65 percent of his or her last gross income until the individual became eligible to collect a state pension, typically at age 60 (for women) or age 63 (for men). The state would reimburse the company for 35 percent of that amount if the company replaced him or her with a registered unemployed person, youth, or examined apprentice who otherwise would not have been employed. The minimum age for early retirement under this program was 58. During the first four full years

22. Hunt (1992, p. 38).
23. Kühlewind (1986, pp. 224–26).

that the act was in effect, however, fewer than 25,000 individuals a year retired under these provisions, a much smaller number than predicted by the act's proponents. Various explanations have been offered for the relatively low takeup rate, but one often-cited factor is that, even with the subsidy offered, many employers who wished to place older workers on early retirement found it more attractive to have them take advantage of the special rules concerning unemployment benefit and early eligibility for a state pension just described.[24]

Pension rules were liberalized to allow many workers to retire early in the 1970s and 1980s because of a disability or a handicap. Workers may qualify for a disability pension at any age; the law only requires that they have contributed to the pension system for at least five years. Decisions by the courts in 1969 and 1976 expanded the definition of disability and greatly increased the numbers claiming disability pensions.[25] A 1973 law allowed severely handicapped workers with at least thirty-five years of pension fund contributions to retire early at age 62. This age was lowered to 61 in 1979 and to 60 in 1980.

Apprenticeship Training

Germany has a unique system of apprenticeship training, which is widely credited with providing German industry with a highly skilled and flexible work force. Companies recruit apprentices at age 16 or 17 and train them for two to three years. About two-thirds of all teenagers participate in the system.[26] Apprenticeships are offered in all sectors of the economy, in white-collar as well as blue-collar jobs.

Apprenticeship training in Germany is often referred to as the dual system because apprentices receive both on-the-job and classroom training. The system is jointly managed by the employers' associations, the unions, and the government. Apprentices must pass written and oral examinations. To maintain uniform standards, the curriculum for a particular apprenticeship is set at the federal level, and local industry

24. Kühlewind (1986, pp. 224–26).
25. Before these decisions, individuals who were physically able to work part time could not receive a pension. Following the decisions, persons who could work part time but for whom part-time work was not available were eligible for a full pension. In 1985 the law was tightened to require at least three years of unemployment within the last five years. This rule change primarily prevented housewives who had not been in the labor force from collecting disability pensions. See Jacobs, Kohli, and Rein (1987).
26. Münch (1991, p. 41).

chambers conduct examinations. Therefore, the dual system emphasizes general training in a particular skill. Observers of the system have stressed that it also socializes teenagers to a working environment, teaching them the importance of punctuality and reliability. In return for this training, apprentices receive low wages relative to skilled adult workers.

The costs of apprenticeship training are shared by companies and by the state (Länder) and federal governments. Large companies often supplement apprenticeship training in state-supported vocational schools with their own classroom training. State governments typically help support the costs of in-class training by companies. Smaller companies often send apprentices to training centers that are jointly funded by local chambers of commerce and the Federal Ministry of Education and Science (Bundesministerium für Bildung und Wissenschaft).

There is a consensus among German trade unions and employers that the apprenticeship system is important for maintaining German industry's competitiveness in world markets. Germany is highly dependent on exports; during the 1980s about a third of output in the manufacturing sector was exported. Because its work force is highly paid, Germany relies on "quality rather than price-competitive products, and . . . [thus needs] a highly skilled and reliable workforce as well as a cooperative relationship between management and labour on the shop floor."[27]

Some observers have argued that the apprenticeship system provides important labor flexibility to employers. In a system in which adjusting the work force is difficult or costly because of restrictions on dismissals, employers must be able to easily redeploy workers within the company to accommodate changes in demand. The apprenticeship system contributes to such internal flexibility of the work force in two ways. First, firms may use apprentices as a reserve work force, deploying them in various unskilled and semiskilled jobs on an as-needed basis. In return for fairly low pay and flexibility, apprentices receive training and stable employment. Second, the apprenticeship programs are designed to give the work force a broad set of skills. During a downturn an employer may avoid laying off excess workers by reassigning them to positions vacated by workers who quit or retire. Such internal transfers are less costly to a company if workers are broadly trained.[28]

---

27. Streeck (1987, p. 5).
28. For a discussion of this role that the apprenticeship system plays, see Bruche and Reissert (1984).

The apprenticeship system also gives employers additional flexibility in adjusting employment levels to changing demand conditions. Apprentices are not covered by employment protection laws. During a downturn, an employer may easily reduce its work force by not offering permanent contracts to its graduating apprentices. Conversely, if uncertainty occurs over whether an upturn is permanent or transitory, a company may increase its work force at relatively low risk and cost by offering more apprenticeships.

Industrial Relations in the United States

While the set of industrial relations institutions and labor market policies in Germany generally support a system of strong job security, quite the opposite situation exists in the United States. U.S. companies rely extensively on hiring and firing to adjust labor, particularly blue-collar labor, to changing demand conditions. This practice first developed as part of a broader system of industrial relations in unionized establishments in the United States and subsequently spread to the nonunion sector. Arguably, public policies are partly responsible for the development of these labor adjustment practices. Until recently, the United States had imposed no restrictions on layoffs for economic reasons, and the unemployment insurance system in the United States has favored the use of layoffs over work sharing.

Union Representation and Personnel Practices

Unlike Germany, the United States has no legally mandated system of worker representation. In most cases, unions represent the sole vehicle for worker representation in the negotiation of wages, benefits, and personnel policies.

In the United States, union organization and collective bargaining are far more decentralized than in Germany. Unions in the United States comprise a network of strong local unions, numbering about 65,000. Local unions almost always are affiliated with an international union, organized along industry or craft lines. There were 168 international unions in 1982; this number compares with just 16 unions in Germany. Most of the international unions, in turn, are affiliated in the American Federation of Labor–Congress of Industrial Organizations (AFL-CIO), which, like the DGB in Germany, is an umbrella organization with primarily political functions.

Although a large proportion of collective agreements are negotiated between unions and employers associations, multiemployer negotiations are not the dominant form of collective bargaining, as is true in Germany. In 1980 about 40 percent of all collective agreements signed, representing about 43 percent of unionized workers, were multiemployer agreements.[29] Most of these agreements were outside of manufacturing. Most collective agreements are signed between a single employer and a union; frequently contracts apply only to a single plant of a multiplant company. The local union is especially likely to be involved in the negotiation of contracts that cover a single plant.

Trends in union strength have been dramatically different in the United States and Germany. Union density (the percent of the work force that is unionized) declined sharply in the United States in the 1970s and 1980s. In 1970, 31 percent of nonagricultural wage and salary employees in the United States were union members; by 1986, union density had fallen to just 17 percent. In contrast, over the same period union density rose moderately in Germany from 37 percent to 43 percent.[30]

The different trends in unionization in the two countries reflect very different attitudes by management toward unions. In the United States, management has aggressively sought to keep new operations from being unionized and even to drive out unions from already organized establishments through a decertification process. One hypothesis advanced for the decline of unions in the United States that has received considerable empirical support holds that the decline reflects the growth in aggressive, sophisticated antiunion practices that American management has adopted.[31]

While American management has sought to improve industrial relations by eliminating unions, German management, in general, has accepted the role of unions in collective bargaining as legitimate and

29. U.S. Department of Labor (1981, p. 19).
30. These figures were taken from Freeman (1989, p. 130). One needs to be careful in comparing unionization rates across countries. As in the United States, in Germany negotiated contracts typically are applied alike to union members and nonmembers within a firm. And in Germany most employers choose to comply with the relevant contract and the regional or national labor minister formally may extend a collective agreement to cover all companies in an industry. For these reasons, union membership understates the true influence of unions in Germany.
31. Freeman (1989) and Weiler (1983) advance this argument.

has viewed a stable relationship with unions as essential for social peace. This perspective does not imply that the relationship between management and unions is nonadversarial in Germany. In 1986, for example, business interests pushed through restrictive legislation on the right of strikers to collect unemployment insurance benefits that greatly weakened union power. Still, German management basically supports unions and the centralized structure of bargaining that exists in that country. This attitude has been reflected in management behavior during the reunification of East and West Germany. During reunification, employers' associations have been trying to organize businesses into employers' associations in the East, while unions have been trying to reproduce their union organization there. West German employers interviewed for this study universally expressed strong support for these unionization efforts. They preferred the stability of a well-established collective bargaining system to the uncertainty inherent in an environment in which the industrial relations system is ill-defined.

Despite the decline in importance of unions in the United States, unions have had a large influence on personnel practices that persists today, primarily because personnel policies pushed for by unions were widely adopted in nonunion settings following World War II.[32] Most blue-collar work in the United States is characterized by tightly defined jobs with rigid work rules, and wages that are attached to jobs, not to individuals. Because of strict work rules, management has little discretion to redefine the tasks that workers perform. Management may have limited freedom to move workers from one job to another; seniority is usually the principal criterion in promotion decisions.

Another important characteristic of U.S. personnel policies is the absence of job security. Among blue-collar workers, "It is understood that management is free to vary the size of the labor force as it wishes."[33] However, because layoffs usually are determined by inverse order of seniority, an individual acquires job security by virtue of his or her tenure.[34] In the unionized sector, senior workers commonly enjoy extensive bumping rights that allow them to displace less senior workers rather than be laid off themselves. A reduction in force thus may gen-

32. The discussion that follows draws heavily on the description of industrial relations practices in the United States found in Osterman (1988, pp. 60–91).

33. Osterman (1988, p. 64).

34. Abraham and Medoff (1984, 1985) provide evidence on the importance of seniority for decisions affecting nonunion as well as union blue-collar workers in the United States.

erate many job changes, as senior workers whose positions are eliminated displace less senior workers in other positions, who in turn may displace workers junior to themselves. U.S. employers, particularly those who are unionized, make heavy use of temporary layoffs.[35] Collective bargaining agreements typically specify that seniority will govern the order of recall from temporary layoff.

Quite different personnel practices typically apply to salaried workers. Job descriptions and career paths are more flexible. Management is more free to alter the tasks that individuals perform as part of their jobs, ability is a more important criterion in promotion, and merit is a more important criterion in pay than is the case with blue-collar workers. Greater flexibility in job assignment, pay, and promotion goes hand in hand with greater security in employment. While for blue-collar workers, "It is explicitly understood that the firm will adjust the size of the labor force in response to product market conditions or technological change, the implicit premise [for salaried workers] is that layoffs either simply will not occur or that the firm will be strenuous in its effort to avoid them."[36] Anecdotal evidence suggests that, during the most recent recession, companies have become more willing to fire salaried workers. Between July 1990, the start of the most recent recession, and January 1992, seasonally adjusted employment of nonproduction workers in manufacturing fell by 4.0 percent, only slightly less than the 4.9 percent decline in the seasonally adjusted employment of manufacturing production workers.[37] It is as yet unclear, however, to what extent these recent reductions in nonproduction employment reflect a permanent increase in the cyclicality of white-collar employment rather than simply a one-time work force restructuring.

Taken together, rigid job definitions and work rules, wages that are tied to jobs, and entitlement to positions based on seniority give individual blue-collar workers some protection against managerial discretion and some job security in an inherently unstable economic environment. Because of the flexible nature of white-collar work, this avenue of job security is closed to salaried workers. Instead, in what can be seen as a quid pro quo for greater managerial discretion concerning their job assignments, pay, and promotions, these workers have received an im-

35. Medoff (1979) documents the greater use of temporary layoffs by union compared with nonunion employers.

36. Osterman (1988, p. 66).

37. These figures are based on employment data from the Bureau of Labor Statistics' monthly Employment, Payroll, and Hours survey.

plicit commitment that management will try to avoid layoffs even when a cutback might enhance short-term profits.[38]

Interestingly, the personnel practices that have applied to salaried workers in the United States are very similar in concept to the personnel practices that apply more generally to German workers. In Germany, both blue- and white-collar workers receive strong job security and in return management has considerable flexibility to reassign workers across jobs within the firm.

Many U.S. companies—union and nonunion—have experimented with providing their blue-collar work force with job security. Among the nonunion companies, IBM is probably the most prominent example with its promise of no layoffs among its regular work force. In addition, several collective agreements have been negotiated in autos, steel, and farm machinery that contain innovative job security clauses for blue-collar workers. Still, companies with these personnel practices are the exception, not the rule, in the United States, and many of the companies that had been most committed to strong job security have found it difficult to maintain that commitment in recent years.

Advance Notice Legislation

In contrast to Germany, where advance notice of layoff has been required by law since the 1920s, advance notice provisions in U.S. law were first enacted in 1988. Before 1988, only three states—Maine, Wisconsin, and Hawaii—required advance notice of mass layoffs or plant closings.[39] Besides these state laws, some union contracts required advance notification of plant closure or relocations. Of 1,550 major collective agreements in effect on January 1, 1980, 150 required advance notice in one or both of these situations.[40]

In the absence of any national law requiring advance notice, however, workers often received little or no advance warning before being let go. According to the results of a study by the U.S. General Accounting Office, 30 percent of businesses that experienced a mass layoff or plant closing during 1983 or 1984 gave affected blue-collar workers no notice

38. For discussions on the link in personnel practices between flexibility and job security, see Osterman (1988); Piore (1986); and Sengenberger (1985).

39. The Maine law was passed in 1971, the Wisconsin law in 1976, and the Hawaii law in 1987. See Leigh (1989, pp. 83–84) for a more complete description of these state laws.

40. U.S. Department of Labor (1981, p. 107).

of the date they would be laid off, and another 34 percent gave two weeks' notice or less; only 7 percent gave individuals more than ninety days notice. For white-collar workers, 26 percent of the establishments gave individuals no notice and another 28 percent gave two weeks' notice or less; only 10 percent gave notice of more than ninety days.[41] The same study indicated that slightly over half of the responding establishments made severance payments to laid-off white-collar employees, but that only a third made severance payments to laid-off blue-collar employees. Unfortunately, no information was collected on the size of these severance payments.[42]

In 1988 Congress passed the Worker Adjustment and Retraining Notification Act. The law, which took effect in 1989, requires employers to give workers and state and local government officials sixty days' advance notice before a mass layoff or plant closure. In general, a mass layoff is defined as a layoff of at least one-third of the work force at a single site within a thirty-day period or a situation in which at least one-third of the workers have their hours reduced by at least 50 percent for six months.[43] Opponents of the legislation feared that the interpretation of the law—which provides for several exceptions to the advance notice requirements—would result in an explosion of litigation. In the first year after the act took effect, however, very few suits were filed.[44]

The U.S. advance notice law is far weaker than German collective dismissal law. The requirement that employers negotiate a social plan with the works council is widely regarded as the most important in German collective dismissal law. U.S. law lacks any requirement that companies consult with worker representatives or pay compensation to laid-off workers.

Unemployment Insurance System

The unemployment insurance system in the United States is governed by a patchwork of state laws whose rules on the amount and duration

41. The numbers given here are for specific notice, which is defined as notice to individual employees that as of a certain date they will no longer be employed at the establishment.

42. See U.S. General Accounting Office (1986).

43. At least 50 workers must be affected, and therefore small establishments are exempted from any notice requirement. The requirements of advance notice also apply if 500 or more workers are laid off, even if they do not constitute at least one-third of the work force.

44. Samborn (1990).

of benefits vary. These laws specify minimum and maximum benefit levels; the share of a worker's previous income replaced therefore depends on both his or her state of residence and previous wages. Most estimates imply, however, that the average net replacement rate in the United States is far below the 63 percent to 68 percent of net income received by German workers in their first year of unemployment.[45]

Benefits are also paid for a much shorter time in the United States than in Germany. In all but three states, the maximum potential duration of benefits is just twenty-six weeks (Delaware limits the maximum potential duration of benefits to twenty-four weeks, while Massachusetts and Washington allow collection of benefits for up to thirty weeks), and the actual potential duration of benefits for all UI claimants currently averages only about twenty-four weeks.[46]

During recessions and in states where unemployment exceeds certain thresholds, federal programs have increased the maximum potential duration of benefit receipt beyond twenty-six weeks, but these programs have been limited in scope. A permanent program introduced in 1970 allows for the payment of up to thirteen weeks of additional benefits during periods when the national insured unemployment rate or the individual state's insured unemployment rate is sufficiently high. In November of 1991, however, even though the official national unemployment rate had reached 6.9 percent, no state was eligible to make extended benefit payments. New legislation passed in that month loosened the criteria for determining a state's eligibility for the extended benefit program, but the intent is still that benefit periods should be lengthened only when economic conditions are unusually bad. Temporary programs introduced during the 1974–75 recession allowed some unemployment insurance recipients to collect benefits for as long as sixty-five weeks, but these provisions expired in March 1977. A much more limited extension of benefits was in effect between 1982 and 1985.[47] In Germany normal unemployment benefits may be collected for fifty-two weeks; after a year of unemployment, German benefits are

---

45. Burtless (1987, p. 138).

46. National Foundation for Unemployment Compensation and Workers Compensation (1991, pp. 53–54); and U.S. Department of Labor (undated).

47. For additional details about the history of extended benefit programs, see National Commission on Unemployment Compensation (1980) and the chronology of federal unemployment insurance legislation contained in National Foundation for Unemployment Compensation and Workers' Compensation (1991).

subject to a means test but may be received indefinitely by those who qualify.

In the United States unemployment insurance benefits are financed, for the most part, by a payroll tax on employers. An employer's tax rate depends on that employer's layoff experience, among other factors. Therefore, employers who lay off more workers pay higher unemployment insurance taxes. This experience rating of unemployment insurance tax rates is usually imperfect in the sense that the higher tax rate for laying off a worker is less costly to an employer than the amount the individual collects in benefits.

American economists have intensely debated the extent to which this imperfect experience rating has led U.S. employers to rely too heavily on layoffs. In Germany, although unemployment insurance tax rates are not based at all on an employer's layoff rate, the absence of experience rating has generated little policy concern. This lack of concern probably occurs because other policies in Germany substantially inhibit layoffs: advance notice for individuals, compensation to laid-off workers in cases of large-scale layoffs, and a tradition of providing stable employment. In practice, temporary layoffs are virtually unknown in Germany.

For a U.S. employer, the added cost of unemployment insurance associated with laying off a worker depends on three things: the amount of the worker's weekly benefits; the duration of receipt of benefits; and the share of benefits for which the employer ultimately pays through higher unemployment insurance taxes. Weekly benefits average roughly 35 percent of gross weekly wages; the average duration of benefits varies somewhat over the business cycle but has typically been about fourteen weeks; and, at the margin, a typical employer bears perhaps 60 percent of the cost of benefits paid to laid-off workers (though many employers are already paying the maximum unemployment insurance tax rate and thus incur no additional costs if they lay off more workers). Thus, a rough estimate of the cost to a typical employer of laying off another worker is about three weeks' wages in the form of increased unemployment insurance tax liability.[48]

48. *Unemployment Insurance Financial Data*, published by the U.S. Department of Labor, contains data on weekly benefit amounts, weekly wages in covered employment, and the duration of benefit receipt. Vroman (1989) discusses alternative estimates of the degree of experience rating. The share of benefits to laid-off workers typically paid for by their employers at the margin may be as low as 50 percent or as high as 75 percent, but using either of these figures in place of the 60 percent figure assumed in

It is difficult to say how this cost compares with the severance costs faced by the typical German firm. When a layoff is large enough to be considered a collective dismissal under German law, the German employer's severance costs probably would be much larger than the U.S. employer's costs. As discussed earlier, the median severance payment in social plans negotiated between 1980 and 1985 amounted to about seventeen weeks' wages. However, in a layoff that is not considered a collective dismissal, the German employer is required to make no severance payment and incurs no increase in unemployment insurance tax liability. Data reported in one study indicate that, in 1978, German employers made severance payments in only one-third of all dismissals (economic and noneconomic) and that the median severance payment was only 2,700 DM.[49]

Short-Time Compensation Programs

Another important difference between the U.S. and German unemployment insurance systems concerns their coverage of short-time work. Although all states offer partial unemployment benefits, these programs do not support work-sharing schemes that might be used by an employer to avert layoffs because in most states workers' earnings must be very low before they qualify for the receipt of benefits. Typically, the benefits received equal the weekly benefit amount minus wages earned during the week net of an allowance or "earnings disregard." Consequently, in most states for earnings above this disregard level, the marginal tax rate is 100 percent.[50] The primary purpose of partial unemployment insurance programs in the United States is to provide some protection for workers whose earnings drop well below their normal level, rather than to encourage work sharing.[51]

In contrast, under short-time compensation (STC) programs workers receive a fraction of full weekly benefits, where the fraction is the

---

the text would not much affect our estimate of the unemployment insurance cost of a layoff.

49. Falke and others (1981, pp. 132 ff).

50. In a handful of states, the earnings disregard is calculated as a fraction of wages, but even in these states persons earning more than a low multiple of the weekly benefit amount are typically not eligible to collect partial unemployment benefits. See National Foundation for Unemployment Compensation and Workers Compensation (1991, pp. 56–57).

51. For a discussion of this point, see Hamermesh (1978).

proportion of hours lost because of work sharing. In Germany unemployment compensation for workers who are working shorter hours owing to a fall in demand is a well-established program, but in the United States prorated benefits for workers on short time were only recently introduced and are still not universally available. As of the beginning of 1991 fourteen states allowed such payments.[52]

In all states with STC programs, a work-sharing plan must be agreed upon by the employer, union (if present), and state employment security agency. Unlike in Germany, states usually require that an STC program be reapproved if any aspect changes. The duration of benefits is typically limited to between twenty and thirty weeks, depending on the state. State laws require that some minimum percentage—between 10 percent and 20 percent—of the work force be affected before the firm can apply for compensation for short time. Certain states also limit receipt of short-time compensation to between 40 percent and 50 percent of the work force. Although most state laws do not require employers to maintain fringe benefits, survey evidence shows that most employers choose to do so.[53]

Because of concern about the effects of paying short-time compensation on states' trust fund balances, the first STC laws passed all contained special provisions under which placement of workers on short time was treated less favorably than placement of workers on temporary layoff. As greater experience with STC programs has been acquired, some of these provisions have been dropped.[54] As of the beginning of 1991, however, half of the fourteen states with STC programs still had special financing provisions or limitations on the use of STC that did not apply to regular unemployment benefits.

In three states (Florida, Missouri, and Oregon), employers using work-sharing schemes may be assessed a higher tax rate than the maximum rate for non-work-sharing employers. In one state (Arizona) employers who use work sharing are assessed an additional tax if they have a negative reserve balance, and in another (Massachusetts) an employer whose account reserve percentage is negative will be charged on a dollar-for-dollar basis for benefits paid out under work sharing. Two states

---

52. These states are Arizona, Arkansas, California, Florida, Kansas, Louisiana, Maryland, Massachusetts, Missouri, New York, Oregon, Texas, Vermont, and Washington.
53. Kerachsky and others (1985).
54. Vroman (1990).

(Arkansas and Kansas) prohibit employers with negative account balances from using STC programs.[55] In all of these seven states, therefore, the unemployment insurance system still favors the use of layoffs over work sharing, at least for certain employers.

Thus far, use of short-time compensation by employers in states with STC programs has been extremely low in comparison with its use in Germany and other countries. The costs of maintaining fringe benefits and tax penalties or other limitations on the use of short time are two possible reasons for its low usage.

Apprenticeship Training

We emphasized the important role that formal training, especially apprenticeship training, plays in providing a skilled and flexible work force in Germany. No such comprehensive system of training exists in the United States. According to one estimate, German companies spend roughly twice as much per worker on training as do U.S. companies.[56]

These differences in private sector spending on training are accounted for, in large part, by differences in spending on apprenticeship training. Apprenticeship programs have been declining in relative importance in the United States. Over half of the apprenticeships offered in the United States are in the unionized construction industry. In 1988, only about 3 percent of American 25-year-olds who had not graduated from college had participated in an apprenticeship program, whereas roughly two-thirds of German youth receive apprenticeship training.[57]

While apprenticeship training is far more important in Germany than in the United States, vocational training undertaken by workers on their own initiative is much more common in the United States than in Germany. Although very few U.S. young people have participated in apprenticeship programs, nearly a third of those without a college degree have participated in some kind of formal off-the-job training, most typically courses offered by private proprietary institutions.[58] In

---

55. National Foundation for Unemployment Compensation and Workers' Compensation (1991, p. 58). Information for Arkansas was taken directly from that state's Employment Security Law on Shared Work Unemployment Compensation.

56. Cited in Hilton (1991, p. 33).

57. Data on participation in apprenticeship programs by U.S. youth are reported by Blanchflower and Lynch (1991). For more general discussions of apprenticeship training programs in the United States and comparisons with those in Germany, see U.S. Congress (1990) and Hilton (1991).

58. Blanchflower and Lynch (1991, p. 27).

addition, a great number of working adults enroll in vocationally oriented community college courses.[59] A worker-driven training system of the sort that arguably exists in the United States has certain advantages. Nonetheless, the training that most U.S. workers receive is likely to be less systematic and less well designed to meet employers' long-term needs than the preparation that would be provided by a well-structured apprenticeship system.

In recent years the U.S. Department of Labor has made some efforts to strengthen traditional apprenticeship programs and promote apprenticeships in nontraditional industries through demonstration programs. Congress has shown great interest in developing policies that would encourage the expansion of apprenticeship programs. To date, however, government funding for apprenticeship programs has been limited.

The Effects of Institutions on Labor Market Adjustment

On the basis of labor market institutions in the United States and Germany, we might expect employers in the two countries to respond to product market changes in very different ways. German regulations discourage employers from laying off workers during downturns. Because it is difficult for German employers to lay off workers when demand declines, employers also are likely to be cautious about hiring new workers during an expansion until they are certain that the increase in demand is not transitory. Though these regulations inhibit layoffs, other German policies encourage the adjustment of average hours per worker and ease the cost to employers of providing stable employment for their work force. During a downturn, a company may apply for unemployment insurance benefits for workers on short time. Moreover, companies are not penalized with a higher tax rate for placing workers on short time, as they may be in American states with short-time compensation programs.

The German apprenticeship system also helps ease the cost to employers of strong job security policies. Apprentices are exempt from protection under Germany's dismissal laws; therefore, employers may use the apprenticeship program to screen job candidates at relatively low cost. Perhaps more important, the apprenticeship program provides workers with a broad set of skills. This type of training makes it less

59. Hamilton (1990, pp. 102–03).

costly for employers to avoid laying off excess workers by transferring them into positions vacated by those quitting or retiring.

Government regulation of layoffs is a more recent phenomenon in the United States and is still much more limited than in Germany. Policies that ease the costs to companies of using alternatives to layoff, such as unemployment insurance for short-time work and government-subsidized early retirement programs, are either absent or present in only limited ways in the United States. Based on these institutional differences, we might expect that over short periods American employers would rely more on the adjustment of employment levels and less on the adjustment of average hours per worker in response to demand changes than would German employers. How long such differences in employment and hours adjustment would persist is unclear.

Differences in labor market institutions in the United States and Germany also may have important implications for how the burden of adjustment is distributed across groups of workers. In principle, the greater use of work sharing in Germany should result in a more equal distribution of adjustment across workers there than in the United States. In both countries, however, certain groups of workers might be expected to bear the brunt of adjustment to downturns.

In the United States we would expect younger age groups to bear the brunt of adjustment because individuals typically are selected for layoff on the basis of last-in, first-out policies, and because youth make up the largest component of new entrants to the labor force. In Germany, the effects of labor adjustment policies on youth are less clear-cut. German youth may be less vulnerable to layoff than U.S. youth because layoffs are less common and seniority is a less important criterion in determining who is to be laid off. Yet, German youth may be particularly hard hit by hiring freezes as a way of reducing the work force. Older workers are likely to absorb a disproportionate amount of any adjustment that occurs in Germany because of the government's extensive support for various early retirement programs, though at least in principle participation in such programs is voluntary.

In both countries a disproportionate amount of adjustment to product demand changes is likely to fall on women. Women are more inclined to interrupt their careers, and therefore, on average, have less tenure than men. To the extent that seniority is a criterion for selecting individuals for layoff, women are more vulnerable. Moreover, women trying to reenter the labor force, much like youth trying to find their first job, are likely to be especially affected when the economy is weak. In Germany, laws that require employers to take social factors—such as any dependents that a worker may have—into account when choosing individuals for layoff may work to the disadvantage of women, as they may be regarded as secondary wage earners. Finally, because female workers tend to hold the less-skilled jobs and therefore have less firm-specific human capital, they may be more vulnerable to layoff, since employers are more willing to let their less-skilled workers go during downturns. This factor may be reinforced in Germany by requirements that employers pay compensation to laid-off workers in the event of a collective dismissal. Compensation depends, among other things, on how long a worker has been with the firm. Because women, on average, have lower tenure than men, it tends to be less costly for German employers to lay off women.

CHAPTER THREE

An Overview of Labor Market Performance in Germany and the United States

I S THE SET OF German labor market institutions described in chapter 2 a model for the United States to emulate or to avoid? Somewhat paradoxically, over the last two decades, German labor market institutions alternately have been portrayed as a model for strong growth with low inflation, on the one hand, and as a major cause of economic stagnation and high unemployment, on the other. These changing assessments of German labor market institutions have typically been tied to the country's macroeconomic performance. Following the first oil price shock in the mid-1970s, Germany experienced moderate unemployment and inflation compared with the United States and many other European countries. During this period, German labor market institutions were hailed for their flexibility in accommodating large shocks.[1]

During the 1980s, however, the German economy, like many others in Europe, experienced slow growth and a steep rise in unemployment. German labor market institutions, like those in other European countries, were portrayed as inflexible and responsible for Germany's stagnating employment growth. According to one view, regulations on dismissals contributed to the rise in German unemployment by making employers more hesitant to hire new workers.

Beginning in the late 1980s the German economy rebounded with high growth in output and employment and falling unemployment. As the U.S. and other industrial economies slipped into recession in 1990,

---

1. A good example of this line of argument is contained in Flanagan, Soskice, and Ulman (1983, pp. 208–300). Sachs (1979) argues that the structure of wage setting in Germany influenced monetary policy in the 1970s and resulted in lower inflation and moderate wage increases.

the newly reunified Germany maintained strong growth. Correspondingly, public images of the strength of German institutions have become more positive.

Clearly, aggregate trends cannot tell us about the specific effects of labor market institutions on economic performance—too many other factors affect the economy. Still they can be indicative. If an economy has experienced prolonged strong growth and low unemployment, that suggests its labor market institutions are at least compatible with good economic performance. Conversely, if an economy experiences low growth and high unemployment for a prolonged period, that signals a warning about the viability of those institutions.

In this chapter, we review broad trends in the labor market in Germany and the United States since the 1970s. Although economic conditions in Germany improved dramatically by the late 1980s, our analysis focuses on the earlier years of that decade. During much of the 1980s, the German economy experienced its weakest performance in comparison with that of the United States, and during this period German labor market institutions, including job security policies, came under their sharpest attack from academics, business leaders, and policymakers. Many observers have drawn misleading conclusions about the labor market performance of the German and U.S. economies, exaggerating the problems of the German economy by using data that are not comparable across countries. In particular, German unemployment rates were about the same as or lower than those in the United States during the 1980s, not higher as many have supposed.

German unemployment did rise precipitously in the 1980s. We review explanations for that rise, including the possible adverse effects of various labor market policies.

Macroeconomic Trends in the 1970s and 1980s

During the 1970s the trend growth of real output in Germany and the United States was similar. During the 1980s, however, patterns of growth in the two countries diverged. Although the United States experienced a more severe recession in the early 1980s, it also experienced a sharper recovery, and for the 1980s overall trend growth in real GNP was higher in the United States than in Germany (table 3-1). In recent years the U.S. economy again has experienced a more severe recession than the German economy.

Table 3-1. *Trends in GNP and the Current Account Balance, 1970–89*

Year	Annual growth of real GNP (percent)		Balance on current account (billions of dollars)	
	United States	Germany	United States	Germany
1970	−0.3	5.0	2.33	0.87
1971	2.8	3.0	−1.43	0.80
1972	5.0	4.2	−5.98	1.20
1973	5.2	4.7	7.15	5.02
1974	−0.5	0.2	1.96	10.55
1975	−1.3	−1.4	18.13	4.33
1976	4.9	5.6	4.21	3.71
1977	4.7	2.7	−14.51	4.01
1978	5.3	3.3	−15.44	8.90
1979	2.5	4.0	−1.00	−5.41
1980	−0.2	1.5	1.37	−13.82
1981	1.9	0.0	8.95	−3.55
1982	−2.5	−1.0	−7.08	5.11
1983	3.6	1.9	−39.58	5.30
1984	6.8	3.3	−98.36	9.81
1985	3.4	1.9	−122.38	16.42
1986	2.7	2.3	−152.99	39.20
1987	3.7	1.7	−159.55	45.17
1988	4.4	3.6	−125.55	48.54
1989	3.0	4.0	—	—

Source: *OECD Economic Outlook* (June 1987, p. 168); and (June 1990, pp. 181, 200).

Despite lower overall growth in the German economy during the 1980s, German export performance was strong. While the United States developed a large deficit on its current account beginning in the mid-1980s, Germany developed a large surplus. The large German current account surplus occurred entirely because of the strength of merchandise exports, where the surplus of exports over imports was even larger.

Germany also benefited from generally high productivity growth in the 1970s and 1980s compared with the United States. For the business sector overall, the United States experienced no growth in labor productivity, as measured by output per person employed, between 1973 and 1979, while labor productivity increased at an annual rate of 3.1 percent in Germany. Between 1979 and 1988 the rate of growth of labor productivity was just 0.8 percent in the United States compared with 1.6 percent in Germany. German productivity growth in the manufacturing sector was also greater than that in the United States during the 1970s, though it slowed in the first part of the 1980s. Between 1973 and 1979 labor productivity in manufacturing grew at an annual rate of 3.2 percent in Germany and 1.0 percent in the United States; between 1979 and 1988 it grew at a rate of 1.0 percent a year in Germany and 3.8 percent a year in the United States.[2]

Comparing labor markets, German performance was weaker, particularly in the 1980s. For most of the postwar period unemployment rates in Germany were negligible and were much lower than those in the United States. Following the 1982 recession, however, employment expanded rapidly and the unemployment rate dropped sharply in the United States, while employment growth remained slow and unemployment soared in Germany. Many politicians, journalists, and even scholars began to refer to the prolonged expansion in the United States as the American job miracle. The differences in employment growth in the United States and Europe spurred many researchers on both sides of the Atlantic to ask what Americans were doing right and what the Europeans, including the Germans, were doing wrong.[3]

The focus on employment growth, however, exaggerates the differences in the labor market performance of the U.S. and German economies during the 1980s. Changes in the employment-to-population ratio are arguably a better measure of an economy's health than changes in the absolute number of people employed. From 1982 (which represents the trough of the recession) to 1989 employment grew by 17.9 percent in the United States compared with 3.9 percent in Germany, a difference of 14 percentage points. The working age population, however, was growing much faster in the United States than in Germany; from 1982 to 1989 the working age population in the United States expanded by 8.2 percent, while the working age population in Germany grew by just 3.4 percent. Comparing the change in employment-to-population ratios over the period shows Germany in a more favorable

2. Productivity figures on the business sector come from the Organization for Economic Cooperation and Development (1990, p. 126). The business sector refers to the whole economy, excluding the public sector. According to OECD figures, the growth of total factor productivity in the business sector was also much higher in Germany than in the United States during the 1970s and 1980s. Productivity figures for the manufacturing sector come from the authors' calculations based on numbers in U.S. Department of Labor, Bureau of Labor Statistics (1991). According to BLS estimates, labor productivity, as measured by output per hour worked, followed similar patterns as output per person employed in Germany and the United States in the 1970s and early 1980s. By the late 1980s, however, output per hour had again begun to grow much faster in Germany than in the United States.

3. Lawrence and Schultze (1987) and Lindbeck (1985) are good examples of such studies.

light. The United States experienced a 9.0 percent increase in its employment-to-population ratio, compared with a 0.5 percent increase in Germany, a difference of 8.5 percentage points or about 40 percent less than the differential in German and U.S. employment growth rates.[4]

Even comparisons based on the employment-to-population ratio may be misleading. In Germany, the rate of growth of employment basically kept pace with the rate of growth of the working age population, whereas in the United States employment grew much faster than population. Some of the increase in the employment-to-population ratio in the United States relative to that in Germany may reflect supply-side factors, such as changing preferences toward work by women, youth, and older workers in the two countries. The effects of these supply-side decisions are, however, difficult to sort out from those of demand-side factors.

Comparison of official unemployment rates for Germany and the United States can give a misleading picture because German unemployment statistics are based on a different definition of unemployment, which tends to significantly overstate unemployment relative to U.S. concepts.[5] Table 3-2 presents unemployment rates in the United States and Germany from 1970 to 1991. For Germany, table 3-2 gives both official German numbers and numbers adjusted by the U.S. Bureau of Labor Statistics to approximate U.S. concepts. Using either measure, German unemployment rates were far below U.S. rates until the early 1980s. Based on official German figures several researchers have concluded that the German rate rose significantly above the U.S. rate beginning in the mid-1980s.[6] But the adjusted numbers show that, in·fact, unemployment rates were virtually identical in the two countries.

4. These calculations are based on civilian employment and population statistics published in the U.S. Department of Labor, Bureau of Labor Statistics (1992). The BLS makes slight adjustments to the employment numbers from the German Microzensus to make them comparable to the U.S. employment numbers.

5. The official German unemployment rate is calculated by dividing the number of persons registered as unemployed by an estimate of the labor force based on the Mikrozensus, an annual household survey. Persons registered as unemployed need not be actively seeking work. In addition, the registered unemployed include persons with part-time jobs who would like full-time work and others who did some paid work during the week of the registration count. Persons seeking fewer than nineteen hours of work per week are not counted as unemployed.

6. Soltwedel (1988, p. 153); Flanagan (1987, p. 177); and Blanchard and Summers (1988, p. 309) are a few examples.

Table 3-2. *Trends in Unemployment Rates, 1970–91*
Percent of labor force

		Germany	
Year	United States	Adjusted to approximate U.S. concepts	Official German rates
1970	4.9	0.5	0.7
1971	5.9	0.6	0.8
1972	5.6	0.7	1.1
1973	4.9	0.7	1.2
1974	5.6	1.6	2.6
1975	8.5	3.4	4.7
1976	7.7	3.4	4.6
1977	7.1	3.4	4.5
1978	6.1	3.3	4.3
1979	5.8	2.9	3.8
1980	7.1	2.8	3.8
1981	7.6	4.0	5.5
1982	9.7	5.6	7.5
1983	9.6	6.9	9.1
1984	7.5	7.1	9.1
1985	7.2	7.2	9.3
1986	7.0	6.6	9.0
1987	6.2	6.3	8.9
1988	5.5	6.3	8.7
1989	5.3	5.7	7.9
1990	5.5	5.0	7.2
1991	6.7	4.4	6.3

Source: U.S. Department of Labor (1992, pp. 4, 21, and 31).

The Causes of High German Unemployment

Still, the German economy did display a disturbing trend increase in unemployment that in and of itself is important. Although there is little consensus among economists and policymakers on the reasons for the rapid rise in German unemployment, there is no dearth of hypotheses.

Some researchers have laid at least some of the blame for the growth in unemployment on overly cautious macroeconomic policy. They view the problem as arising from insufficient aggregate demand, warranting a Keynesian-style expansionary fiscal policy. However, German policymakers were unwilling to accept the risks of igniting inflation or running large budget deficits.[7]

7. For discussions of this argument see Sachs (1979); Lawrence and Schultze (1987, pp. 10–11); and Lindbeck (1985).

Other observers have cited rigidities in German capital markets that may have resulted in low investment and contributed to the overall weakness in aggregate demand. In particular, it is argued that harsh bankruptcy laws have been hostile to small firms and entrepreneurs and have stifled new investment.[8]

Most analyses of the growth in unemployment, however, have focused on problems in the labor market. Statistically, the growth in unemployment was caused not by an increase in the rate of inflows into unemployment but rather by a decrease in the rate of outflows from unemployment.[9] Many researchers have proposed that various rigidities in the labor market have made employers more reluctant to hire workers.

One of the most commonly held explanations for the growth in German unemployment is excessive wage levels. According to this hypothesis, wages were too high following the oil price shocks in 1974 and 1975 and in 1979 and 1980. In response, businesses reduced capacity and switched to more capital-intensive methods of production. As a result, the German economy, though experiencing high unemployment, was operating at high rates of capacity utilization in the 1980s.[10]

Some analysts have hypothesized that the unemployment problem has to do not only with the level of wages but also with the structure of wages. The highly centralized wage bargaining system in Germany, it is argued, results in relatively narrow wage differentials across business sectors and regions of the country. Consequently, wages in depressed regions of the country and in depressed industries are too high to absorb excess labor. In a variant of this argument, Michael C. Burda and Jeffrey D. Sachs posit that an economy can still retain high employment growth and low unemployment levels if wages in at least one sector of the economy are flexible.[11] In the United States, they argue, even though wages in manufacturing were rigid during the downturns of the 1970s and 1980s, excess labor was absorbed by the services sector. In Germany, the argument continues, wage differentials between manufacturing and

8. For a summary of this view, see Lawrence and Schultze (1987, p. 5).
9. Schettkat (1992, pp. 142–43) presents data on the trends in the unemployment inflow rate and the completed duration of unemployment spells. Changes in the completed duration of unemployment spells reflect changes in the unemployment outflow rate.
10. See OECD (1985, pp. 55–56); Soltwedel (1988); and Lindbeck (1985). Sachs (1983, p. 282) and Schultze (1987, p. 244) provide estimates of the wage gap in Germany.
11. Burda and Sachs (1987).

services are insufficiently large for the services sector to absorb the excess labor from manufacturing. The overly high wages in the services sector may be attributed to a centralized wage bargaining system that sets wage levels too high in that sector, as Burda and Sachs claim, or to a reluctance by industrial workers who have been laid off to accept lower paying service sector jobs.[12]

Demographic factors are another possible source of the growth of unemployment in Germany in the 1980s. Some have been quick to dismiss the idea that labor supply factors contributed significantly to the growth of unemployment in Germany because the overall increase in the labor force was negligible when employment was rising.[13] However, the demographic composition of the labor force changed substantially during the period, shifting toward less-experienced workers. In the late 1970s and 1980s the German economy had to absorb its own baby boom, which was entering the work force. In addition, marked growth occurred in the labor force participation rates of prime-age females.

Economists have also looked for a change in the structure of jobs in the economy that could have created a substantial mismatch between demand and supply in the labor market. The Beveridge curve describes the inverse relationship observed empirically between the rate of job vacancies and the rate of unemployment in the economy. As the vacancy rate increases, the unemployment rate would be expected to fall, all else the same. Wolfgang Franz has shown that the Beveridge curve for Germany shifted out during the 1970s and early 1980s; that is, for any given vacancy rate in the economy, the unemployment rate increased over the period.[14]

Various explanations for this outward shift are possible. One natural hypothesis is that the composition of jobs has changed, resulting in a mismatch of occupational skills demanded and supplied in the economy. Alternatively, there might have been a relative shift in economic activity across regions, resulting in a geographic mismatch between demand growth and labor supply. However, the evidence on occupational and regional mismatch is ambiguous. Franz and Robert J. Flanagan report

12. OECD (1987, p. 33).
13. OECD (1985, p. 49).
14. See Franz (1986). To arrive at this conclusion Franz adjusted official vacancy and unemployment statistics to make them more inclusive. Analyses based on uncorrected data (as contained in OECD [1985] and Blanchard [1989]) show little if any outward shift in the Beveridge curve during that period.

evidence suggesting that the degree of regional mismatch did not increase from the late 1970s to the early 1980s as the unemployment rate was rising sharply.[15] In a 1986 study, Franz reports a measure of occupational mismatch that similarly suggests no increase over the period, though in a later study he notes that the discrepancy between the share of unemployment accounted for by unskilled workers and the share of vacancies for unskilled workers rose substantially between 1976 and 1988.[16] Flanagan, using industry data, presents evidence to suggest that some of the growth in unemployment in Germany may have been caused by a failure of workers leaving declining industries to find employment in expanding industries.[17]

The unemployment rate is a function of the flow of workers into unemployment and the average duration of unemployment spells. As already noted, the duration of unemployment in Germany rose dramatically from the late 1970s to the mid-1980s. By the mid-1980s, nearly a third of all persons registered as unemployed had been out of work for a year or longer.[18] Some have speculated that the rise in long-term unemployment may be an indication that temporary, negative shocks to the German economy had persistent, adverse effects. Following an initial shock some individuals become unemployed. The longer these individuals are unemployed, the more their job skills depreciate and the harder it becomes for them to find new jobs. The long-term unemployed may have difficulty finding new employment even when economic conditions improve. In this way, a "qualifications" mismatch arises, and one-time, temporary shocks to the economy may have lasting, adverse effects on unemployment. Franz and Olivier J. Blanchard and Lawrence H. Summers have suggested that this type of hysteresis process may explain some of the trend increase in unemployment in Germany.[19]

Aspects of the welfare state have also been blamed for the rise in unemployment in Germany. A leading suspect in this area has been the unemployment insurance system, which provides more generous benefits for a longer time than does the system in the United States. According to critics of Germany's generous unemployment insurance benefits, unemployed workers will be under less financial pressure to find new jobs, resulting in an increase in the average duration of unemployment and

15. Franz (1986, p. 35); and Flanagan (1987, p. 183).
16. Franz (1986, p. 35, 1991, p. 119).
17. Flanagan (1987).
18. Bundesanstalt für Arbeit (1991, p. 760).
19. Franz (1986); and Blanchard and Summers (1988).

consequently the unemployment rate. However, if generous unemployment benefits are to explain the increase in the unemployment rate over time, then unemployment benefits must have a greater effect on search behavior during slack markets than during tight markets, or benefits must have become more generous over time. Gary Burtless dismisses the first possibility, arguing instead that generous benefits are likely to have a greater effect on search behavior when labor markets are tight.[20] And Franz disputes the second possibility, pointing out that benefits in Germany were falling at the same time that the unemployment rate was rising.[21]

Employment Protection Laws as a Cause of Unemployment

Of particular importance for the discussion in this book is the allegation that the regulation of layoffs is partly responsible for the rise in unemployment. Opponents of employment protection laws have noted that Germany, like a number of other European countries, greatly strengthened its laws' provisions on the eve of the first oil price shock in the mid-1970s. The effects of such legislation might be expected to be minimal in an economy experiencing rapid and prolonged economic expansion—conditions that characterized postwar Germany until the mid-1970s. Yet, they might be expected to have more adverse effects in the slow-growth economy that prevailed in the 1970s and 1980s. Opponents of the German legislation have argued that the new laws hampered industry's ability to restructure, shed excess labor, and hence compete in world markets. The argument follows that the laws have made employers more cautious in hiring new workers, and in this way contributed to the rise in German unemployment in the 1980s.

Theoretically, a law that increases the cost of laying off a worker to an employer raises the expected costs of hiring a new worker and thus lowers the equilibrium level of employment in the economy over the business cycle, all other things held constant. During a recession, however, employment levels may be higher with protective laws, because although the laws may inhibit new hires, during downturns they may also slow layoffs, and the net effect on employment levels is ambiguous.[22]

20. Burtless (1987, pp. 153–54).
21. Franz (1986, p. 41).
22. See Gavin (1986) and Flanagan (1987, p. 198) on this point.

Moreover, the equilibrium level of employment or employment growth may not be lower if other factors compensate employers for the higher costs of layoffs. For example, the assertion that employment protection laws lower employment assumes that the cost to employers of greater job security is not passed back to workers in the form of lower wages. We will argue in subsequent chapters that although employment protection laws raise the cost of reducing the work force through layoffs, other aspects of public policy and the industrial relations system lower the cost of reducing labor input by other means. In addition, greater job security may increase labor productivity and lower labor costs if, for example, workers are more receptive to change and accept greater flexibility of work assignments within the company.[23] Finally, advance notice requirements, which represent one important form of regulation of layoffs, may increase employment by reducing the duration of unemployment if workers use the period to search for new jobs.

Although economists and policymakers often assume that employment protection laws reduce employment, hard evidence on the effects of these laws is scant. Often the extent to which employment protection laws inhibit layoffs has been exaggerated. An OECD study notes that if one subtracts the recall rate from the layoff rate for the United States, the resulting figures are similar to layoff rates in countries where layoffs are regulated and temporary layoffs are uncommon.[24] Turnover data for Germany do not exist to allow direct comparison of layoff rates in Germany and the United States. However, Flanagan shows that the percent of unemployment resulting from dismissal is quite similar in the two countries.[25]

Those who assert that these laws adversely affect employment implicitly are assuming that they raise the fixed cost of labor to employers. If the fixed cost of hiring a worker rises, employers would be expected to increase the number of hours worked per employee and reduce the number of employees. More general studies of the effects of higher fixed labor costs on the substitution of hours for employment suggest, however, that the impacts are small empirically. According to one summary of the evidence, "large increases in the ratio of fixed to variable labour costs produce only small falls in the employment-hours ratio."[26]

23. For arguments about labor flexibility and productivity, see OECD (1986) and Osterman (1988).
24. OECD (1986, p. 58).
25. Flanagan (1987, p. 196).
26. OECD (1986, p. 21).

Although most analyses have focused on the costs of dismissing workers imposed by employment protection laws in Europe, certain policies in the United States may penalize employers for laying off workers. Unlike the German unemployment insurance system, the U.S. unemployment insurance system is experience rated, so that employers who lay off larger numbers of workers pay higher unemployment insurance taxes. Moreover, U.S. employers may be subject to very large judgments if they are found to have unjustly dismissed a worker, though only a few such cases have been decided to date, and these have not generally involved dismissals occurring in the context of a reduction in force.[27] The average cost of dismissing a worker is probably still higher in Germany than in the United States, but U.S. employers do bear significant dismissal costs.

Conclusion

The employment problems that Germany faced in the 1980s often have been exaggerated when compared with those of the United States. Although employment growth was much lower in the 1980s in Germany than in the United States, the difference in the growth of the two countries' employment-to-population ratios was much less marked. In addition, although the German unemployment rate rose sharply from the 1970s to the 1980s, it began at levels well below the U.S. unemployment rate and peaked at levels that were roughly the same as those in the United States. By the end of the 1980s, the German economy began to grow at a much greater pace and unemployment began to fall sharply, despite the new wave of immigration from Eastern Europe.

Concern about the nature of West Germany's unemployment problem in the 1980s has waned as unemployment there has fallen and as Germany faces the quite different and far more daunting labor market problems posed by reunification. Still, to the extent that the rise in unemployment during the 1980s was caused by misguided policies or by other German institutions that inhibited employment growth, the unemployment problems in the past hold potentially important policy

27. Flanagan (1987, p. 197) cites figures on recent awards in California. In a sample of 102 wrongful discharge cases tried in California between 1982 and 1986, the average jury award for general damages was $344,069, and the average jury award for punitive damages was $557,355.

lessons for the reunification process as well as for the United States and other countries.

Many hypotheses have been proposed to explain the steep rise in unemployment in Germany in the 1980s. Explanations about wage levels, the structure of wages, and the wage bargaining system have probably received the greatest following, although little consensus exists on the extent to which wage rigidities and other factors contributed to the growth in unemployment.

Of greatest interest to the discussion in this book are allegations that employment protection legislation contributed to high levels of unemployment in Germany. As already discussed, the effects of such laws on unemployment are theoretically ambiguous, and the empirical evidence, though quite limited, suggests that any adverse effects are likely to be small.

CHAPTER FOUR

The Effects of Job Security
on Labor Adjustment

T HE ARGUMENT THAT German job security regulations have contributed to lower employment, and higher unemployment, than otherwise would have prevailed rests on the assumption that such regulations
impede employers' ability to adjust labor input during periods of economic contraction. Yet this assumption may often be incorrect. Although German job security regulations may inhibit rapid employment
reductions during downturns, the German unemployment insurance
system subsidizes short-time work. Consequently, German employers
may be better able to adjust hours of work in response to such downturns
than are U.S. employers. In addition, German law creates no bar to
employment reductions over the medium to long run; rather, it requires
only that any use of layoffs to achieve such reductions be discussed with
the works council and that, in the event of a mass layoff, a social plan
to compensate those who are laid off be negotiated. Over the medium
to long run, substantial reductions in employment can be achieved
without layoffs through attrition, hiring freezes, and early retirement
measures.

In this chapter we use data on manufacturing industries in Germany
and the United States to compare employment and hours adjustment in
the two countries. We ask whether the adjustment of employment to
demand changes is typically more sluggish in Germany in the short and
medium run, and if so, whether hours are sufficiently flexible to compensate for the lack of employment adjustment. We also examine the
role that short-time work plays in the adjustment process in Germany
and compare it with the role played by temporary layoffs in the United
States.

Earlier studies comparing adjustment behavior across countries typically have used data for the economy as a whole or for the entire manufacturing sector rather than for more disaggregated industries. Given that important differences may occur in adjustment patterns across industries, analysis of such aggregated data could be misleading. Two previous studies provide evidence on adjustment behavior in the German and U.S. automobile and steel industries, respectively.[1] Both studies conclude that there is substantially less adjustment of employment to output changes in Germany than in the United States, even over a year and a half or more. It turns out, however, that the automobile industry and the steel industry are unrepresentative even of the manufacturing sector. One of our study's contributions is to provide evidence on adjustment behavior in a wider spectrum of manufacturing industries.

Data limitations precluded us from carrying out comparable analyses for nonmanufacturing industries. It should be noted, however, that manufacturing accounts for a disproportionate share of the fluctuations in aggregate output that occur during the typical business cycle and for much of the sectoral realignment that has taken place in Germany and the United States in recent decades. The manufacturing sector is itself diverse, both in its production processes and in the patterns of adjustment observed in the individual industries that we study. Our focus on the manufacturing sector is thus, we believe, much less of a limitation than it might seem to be at first.

Movements in Employment, Hours, and Shipments

To convey basic differences in German and U.S. adjustment behavior, we begin by presenting simple plots of the movements of production worker employment, total production worker hours, and shipments in comparably defined industries in the two countries over time. Figure 4-1 displays a pair of charts, one chart for Germany and one chart for the United States, for each of eleven manufacturing industries. These charts plot the quarter-to-quarter movements in indices of production worker employment, total production worker hours, and the real value of shipments. The charts are based on data from the same sources as those used in fitting econometric models of the responsiveness of pro-

---

1. Köhler and Sengenberger (1983); and Houseman (1988).

duction employment and production hours to changes in shipments.[2] We took care to ensure that the German data and the U.S. data referred to comparably defined industries.[3]

The short-term movements in employment, hours, and shipments displayed in these charts are of particular interest. In Germany, the production worker employment series exhibit little quarter-to-quarter variation, but total hours worked are far more variable. The different behavior of the employment and the total hours series implies that changes in hours per worker account for a significant fraction of the quarter-to-quarter variation in total hours worked. Changes in German shipments are associated with little contemporaneous movement in German employment, but total hours track shipments more closely. In contrast, in the United States, production employment and total production hours move up and down together; considerably less of the quarter-to-quarter variation in total hours worked is accounted for by changes in hours per worker. In most industries, employment tracks shipments more closely in the United States than in Germany, but this pattern generally is not observed for total hours worked. These characterizations are supported by the econometric analyses reported in the following pages.

In many industries, shocks to shipments appear to be less persistent in Germany than in the United States, in the sense that periods of above-trend or below-trend shipments tend to be shorter in duration. Another obvious difference between the German and the U.S. series plotted in figure 4-1 is the much greater volatility of U.S. shipments. In all of the eleven matched manufacturing industries, there is a marked drop in U.S. shipments following the first OPEC oil shock, and another larger drop during the recession of the early 1980s. While German shipments also typically fell following the first OPEC oil shock, these declines typically were less pronounced than those in the United States. Most German manufacturing industries also experienced noticeable declines in shipments during the early 1980s, but these declines tended to be less pronounced than those associated with the first OPEC oil

---

2. German data were available for the period from January 1970 through December 1991, except in the paper industry where complete shipments data were not available after December 1986. Because of changes to the U.S. industrial classification system, data on a consistent basis were available only through July 1990 for the United States.

3. The one exception is the auto industry. The German industry classification, street vehicles, includes motorcycle production, bicycle production and vehicle repair, whereas the U.S. industry classification does not.

Figure 4-1. *Shipments, Production Employment, and Production Hours, Eleven German and U.S. Industries, 1970–90*

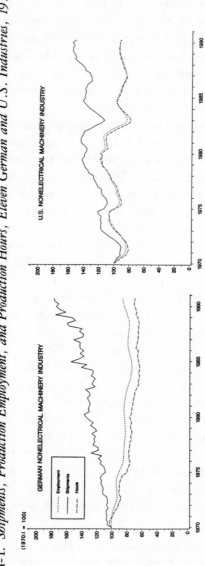

Figure 4-1. *(cont'd)*

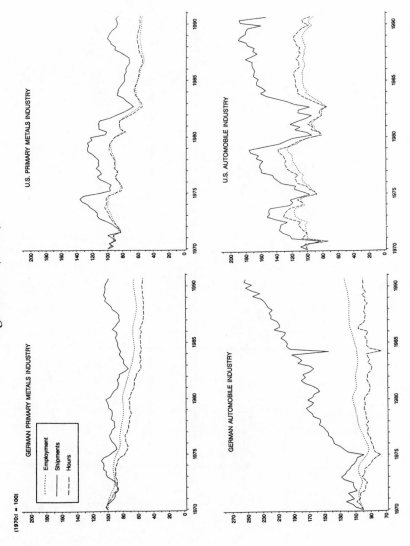

Figure 4-1. (*cont'd*)

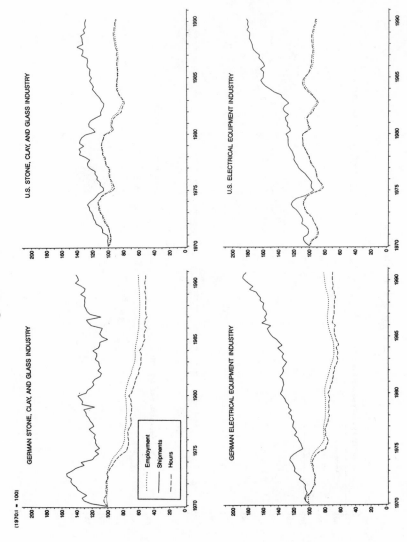

Figure 4-1. (*cont'd*)

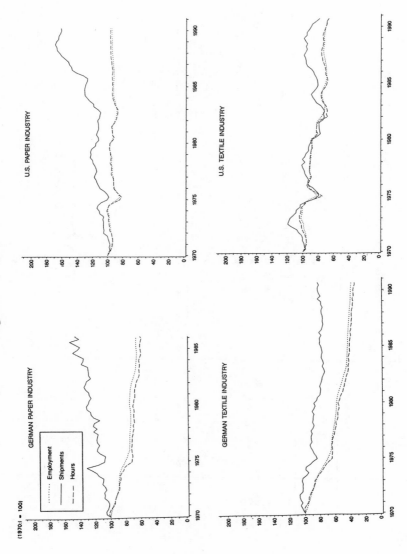

Figure 4-1. (cont'd)

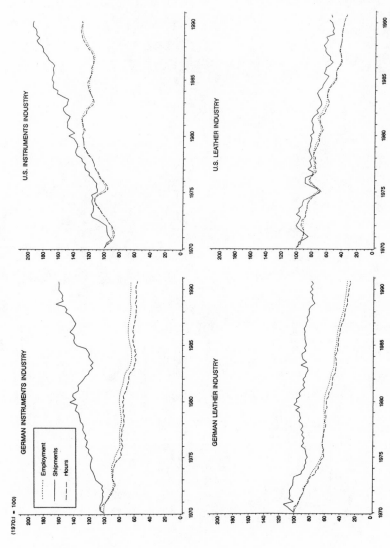

Figure 4-1. *(cont'd)*

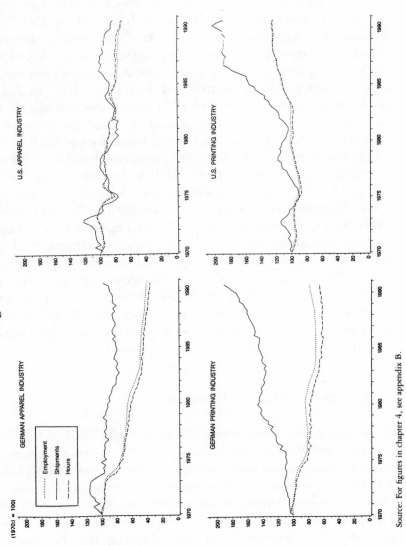

(1970:i = 100)

GERMAN APPAREL INDUSTRY

U.S. APPAREL INDUSTRY

GERMAN PRINTING INDUSTRY

U.S. PRINTING INDUSTRY

- ········ Employment
- ——— Shipments
- —–— Hours

Source: For figures in chapter 4, see appendix B.

shock and smaller than those experienced by the corresponding U.S. industries during the same period. The different experiences of the two countries' manufacturing sectors during the early 1980s reflects, in part, the very strong appreciation of the dollar between 1980 and 1982. The value of the dollar relative to the deutsche mark rose by a third over that two-year period, from 1.82 DM per dollar in 1980 to 2.43 DM per dollar in 1982, thus enhancing the competitiveness of German products on the international market compared with that of U.S. goods.

Whereas the long-run trends in industry shipments, for the most part, have been similar in Germany and the United States, the long-run trends in employment and hours in many industries have been strikingly different. Except in one industry (the automobile industry), employment in each of the eleven German industries was much lower in 1990 than it had been in 1970. The drop in employment tended to be particularly sharp in the 1970s. During the 1980s employment stabilized or even increased slightly in most industries. The relative decline of employment typically has been smaller in U.S. than in German industries. Between 1970 and 1990, total hours of work in Germany fell substantially more than did employment, reflecting a trend decline in the use of overtime and, in certain industries, a decline in the length of the standard work week. No such reduction in weekly work hours occurred in the United States. These trends reflect a larger growth in labor productivity in Germany than in the United States, particularly during the 1970s, whether measured in output per worker or in output per hour worked.

Employment and Hours Adjustment

The primary objective of our empirical analysis is to better understand how labor market institutions affect the dynamic response of employment and hours to short-run changes in labor demand, particularly those changes owing to changes in the demand for output. This task is complicated because employers' labor adjustment decisions depend not only on the institutional structure within which they operate and the magnitude of the associated adjustment costs they face, but also on technological factors and the nature of the short-term variation in the demand for output. The technological environment is important insofar as some technologies permit incremental adjustments in labor input more easily than others. The nature of short-term movements in product demand may influence labor adjustment in at least two ways. First, one would expect labor input to be adjusted more fully to current changes in the demand for output where these changes are relatively long lasting than where they are relatively transitory. Furthermore, if shedding labor through attrition is less costly than shedding labor through layoffs, labor input may be adjusted more fully to small demand changes than to large demand changes.

We attempt to control for the technological environment within which labor adjustment decisions are made by using industry level, rather than aggregate, data in our analysis. Dealing with the potential effect of differences in the structure of demand on labor adjustment in the two countries is less straightforward. As already noted, German and U.S. employers have experienced rather different economic environments since the mid-1970s. Any observed differences between Germany and the United States in the proportional adjustment of labor input to changes in shipments might reflect the response to these differing conditions. The initial estimates of employment and hours adjustment that we present do not control for differences in demand conditions between the two countries. Making use of variation in demand conditions across industries, and the associated cross-industry differences in adjustment patterns, we then endeavor to identify the influence of demand conditions on labor adjustment within each country and adjust our initial estimates to control for cross-country differences in demand conditions. This strategy enables us to assess how adjustment in the two countries would have compared had the economic conditions facing employers been more similar. In general, we conclude that cross-country differences in demand conditions explain little of observed cross-country differences in labor adjustment.

Throughout the analysis, our focus is on the adjustment of an industry's labor input to changes in the demand for its product, as proxied by industry shipments. Quarter-to-quarter changes in product demand are the main source of quarter-to-quarter changes in labor demand. Over the longer term, changes in relative factor prices and changes in productivity influence labor demand, but these factors account for a much smaller share of short- to medium-term labor demand fluctuations.

Here, we adopt a simple model to estimate the adjustment of employment and hours to changes in demand:

$$(4\text{-}1) \quad \ln(N_t) = \Phi_0 + \Phi_1 t + \Phi_2 t^2 + \sum_{s=0}^{6} \theta_s \ln(S_{t-s}) + \epsilon_t \, ,$$

where N represents either production employment or production hours, S represents real shipments (nominal shipments deflated by a price index), t is a time trend term, the Φs and θs are parameters to be estimated, and ϵ is the error term. We use quarterly data to estimate these equations. The sum of the coefficients on, for example, the first three shipments terms in equation 4-1 (the current and the first two lagged values) captures the cumulative response of production employment to a change in shipments over a two-quarter period. Our specification allows changes in shipments to affect employment and hours with a lag of up to six quarters. The time trend coefficients capture anything that might impart a trend to desired labor input, including trends in relative factor prices, productivity, or shipments. Appendix A provides a more detailed discussion of labor adjustment models, comparing our model with other approaches in the literature.

We fit labor adjustment equations for two sets of industries. The first set consists of eleven comparably defined manufacturing industries.[4] Ten of these industries correspond to U.S. two-digit SIC classifications; we also report equations for the German street vehicles industry (SYPRO 33) and the U.S. automobile industry (SIC 371).[5] We took care to identify comparably defined industries because, in drawing cross-country comparisons, we wanted, insofar as possible, to hold constant technological factors that might affect labor adjustment patterns. While the German street vehicles classification differs from the U.S. automobiles classification, we have included results for this industry for comparison with previous studies.

---

4. German and U.S. industries were matched using a bridge of the two countries' industrial classification schemes developed by Hideki Yamawaki.

5. There were various reasons for excluding the remaining two-digit SIC manufacturing industries from our analysis. For lumber, furniture, fabricated metal products, transportation equipment, and miscellaneous durable goods, it was impossible to construct reasonably comparable German and U.S. series. The German petroleum and rubber series were not comparable over time. Finally, the U.S. food, tobacco, and chemicals employment equations behaved so poorly that we felt the estimated coefficients could not be trusted. As explained in appendix B, real shipments series were created for all U.S. industries by deflating nominal shipments by either the durable goods or the nondurable goods producer price index. We suspect that the nondurable goods producer price index is a relatively poor proxy for actual producer prices in food, tobacco, and chemicals. This may account for the poor results in these industries.

The second set of industries for which we fit labor adjustment models includes the most disaggregated industries for which we could obtain the requisite data in each country. This set includes thirty-one manufacturing industries for Germany and forty-nine manufacturing industries for the United States. We use the results for these more disaggregated industries when we examine the effects of differences in demand conditions in Germany and the United States on labor adjustment in the two countries. Further details about the data used in this chapter are provided in appendix B.

The Main Findings

The first set of results we report are based on data for the 1974–84 period. As discussed in chapter 2, significant changes were made to German job security law in the early 1970s. The most important change was the passage of the Works Constitution Act, which took effect in 1973. This act requires that employers try to reach a "compromise of interest" with the works council over any proposed closure or mass dismissal and that employers who carry out a collective dismissal must negotiate a social plan that specifies compensation for laid-off workers. The Employment Promotion Act of 1985 relaxed these regulations on layoffs somewhat. Restricting our attention, at least initially, to the 1974–84 period enables us to compare labor adjustment in Germany and the United States during a period when German job security regulations remained unchanged.

Table 4-1 summarizes the results of our production employment equations; table 4-2 summarizes the results of our production hours equations. In both tables, we have reported selected coefficient sums, beginning with the current shipments coefficient and continuing through the sum of the coefficients on the current plus all six lagged shipments terms. The numbers reported in the first row of table 4-1, for example, imply that a 1.000 percent change in shipments in the German nonelectrical machinery industry leads to a 0.052 percent change in employment in the current quarter, a 0.241 percent change in employment after two quarters and a 0.591 percent change in employment after six quarters if the shock to shipments persists.[6] The tables also indicate the

6. It should be noted that, although the sum of the shipments coefficients over six quarters is in many cases significantly less than one, this fact in itself does not imply increasing returns to scale. This is because employers will not find it in their interests

results of tests on the statistical significance of differences between the German and corresponding U.S. estimates.[7]

Tables 4-1 and 4-2 reveal strikingly different patterns of employment and hours adjustment in the two countries. The production employment estimates in table 4-1 show that, in nine of the eleven matched industries, there is substantially less initial adjustment of employment to changes in shipments in Germany than in the United States. The only exceptions to this general pattern are the apparel and printing industries, in which there is almost no adjustment of employment to changes in shipments in the United States and the current adjustment of employment to shipments, while also small, is actually somewhat larger in Germany.

Within a relatively short time, however, German employment adjustment seems to "catch up" to U.S. employment adjustment. Except in the first four industries listed in the table—nonelectrical machinery, primary metals, automobiles, and stone, clay, and glass—German employment adjustment four to six quarters out is as large as, or even larger than, U.S. employment adjustment. Insofar as the patterns observed can be attributed to the two countries' industrial relations systems, they suggest that requirements for advance notice and the negotiation of a social plan may slow, but do not prevent, employment adjustment.

More relevant to productivity and cost than employers' ability to adjust employment levels, however, is employers' ability to adjust total labor input to changes in demand over the short and medium run. Table 4-2 shows the adjustment of production worker hours, which is the product of production employment and average hours worked per production worker, to changes in shipments. The numbers in this table suggest that the smaller short-run adjustment of German production

---

to fully adjust labor input if demand changes are perceived as temporary and the costs of adjusting labor are high. This point is nicely illustrated in Nickell (1986), especially pp. 485–86. Later in the chapter we explicitly consider the effects that different demand conditions in Germany and the United States may have had on these estimated employment and hours elasticities.

7. The test statistic used in determining the statistical significance of the German-U.S. differences was computed as the difference between the estimated elasticities for the two countries, divided by the square root of the sum of the variances of these elasticities. Under the assumption that the error terms in the U.S. and German equations are uncorrelated, this test statistic has an asymptotic normal distribution. We use the same test statistic for comparisons across time periods.

Table 4-1. *Production Employment Elasticities, 1974–84*

Industry	Current quarter	One quarter	Two quarters	Four quarters	Six quarters
Nonelectrical machinery					
Germany	0.052**	0.129**	0.241**	0.482**	0.591**
United States	0.633	0.907	1.111	1.104	1.211
Primary metals					
Germany	0.039**	0.115**	0.170**	0.260**	0.298**
United States	0.410	0.690	0.688	0.763	0.838
Autos					
Germany	0.097**	0.241**	0.288**	0.444**	0.553
United States	0.445	0.597	0.671	0.730	0.699
Stone, clay, and glass					
Germany	0.070**	0.144**	0.216**	0.396**	0.544
United States	0.260	0.575	0.635	0.764	0.709
Electrical equipment					
Germany	0.188**	0.427**	0.695	1.084	1.101
United States	0.514	0.874	1.022	0.994	0.916
Paper					
Germany	0.099	0.218	0.348	0.531	0.644
United States	0.200	0.395	0.449	0.404	0.535
Textiles					
Germany	0.056	0.169*	0.321	0.629*	0.733
United States	0.197	0.400	0.472	0.317	0.425
Instruments					
Germany	0.102*	0.239*	0.410	0.846	1.002**
United States	0.263	0.482	0.566	0.651	0.623
Leather					
Germany	0.112	0.288	0.470	0.724**	0.704**
United States	0.203	0.360	0.285	0.201	0.058
Apparel					
Germany	0.092	0.264	0.469	0.878**	1.016**
United States	0.030	0.157	0.354	0.328	0.338
Printing					
Germany	0.132*	0.335**	0.439**	0.705**	0.985**
United States	0.027	0.087	0.125	0.163	0.372

Sources: For tables in chapter 4, see appendixes A and B.
**German-U.S. difference significant at 0.05 level, two-tailed test.
*German-U.S. difference significant at 0.10 level, two-tailed test.

Table 4-2. *Production Hours Elasticities, 1974–84*

Industry	Current quarter	One quarter	Two quarters	Four quarters	Six quarters
Nonelectrical machinery					
Germany	0.119**	0.274**	0.373**	0.463**	0.455**
United States	0.761	1.078	1.282	1.079	1.194
Primary metals					
Germany	0.443**	0.466**	0.441**	0.589**	0.552**
United States	0.607	0.915	0.844	0.882	0.950
Autos					
Germany	0.451**	0.568**	0.634**	0.730	0.808
United States	0.639	0.753	0.815	0.825	0.799
Stone, clay, and glass					
Germany	0.280	0.372**	0.470**	0.510**	0.619
United States	0.415	0.820	0.804	0.879	0.812
Electrical equipment					
Germany	0.733	0.811	0.982	1.207	0.939
United States	0.725	1.136	1.219	1.062	1.044
Paper					
Germany	0.265	0.297	0.385	0.409	0.390
United States	0.278	0.569	0.601	0.449	0.700
Textiles					
Germany	0.402	0.397**	0.440	0.754*	0.726
United States	0.484	0.839	0.663	0.403	0.695
Instruments					
Germany	0.280	0.284*	0.381	0.852	0.712
United States	0.376	0.673	0.720	0.748	0.634
Leather					
Germany	0.342	0.561	0.627**	0.826**	0.659**
United States	0.244	0.458	0.295	0.051	−0.093
Apparel					
Germany	0.341	0.504	0.543	1.022**	0.916**
United States	0.101	0.336	0.502	0.431	0.422
Printing					
Germany	0.447**	0.438	0.329	0.482**	0.784**
United States	0.086	0.220	0.236	0.189	0.445

**German-U.S. difference significant at the 0.05 level, two-tailed test.
*German-U.S. difference significant at the 0.10 level, two-tailed test.

employment is largely compensated for by a greater adjustment of German average production worker hours. In seven of the eleven matched industries the adjustment of total German production worker hours to a change in shipments in the current quarter is roughly as much as, or even more than, that of U.S. production worker hours. Even in the four industries where German hours exhibit less contemporaneous adjustment than U.S. hours—nonelectrical machinery, primary metals, automobiles, and stone, clay, and glass—German hours adjustment is much larger than German employment adjustment, and the cross-country differences that were apparent in table 4-1 are much less pronounced in table 4-2.

Taken together, these results suggest that the primary difference between short-run labor adjustment in Germany and that in the United States lies not in the adjustment of total labor input, but rather in its division between employment levels and hours. Particularly in the short run, German industries rely more heavily on the adjustment of average hours per worker. Over the medium run, however, the typical German manufacturing industry adjusts employment levels by as much as the matched U.S. industry.

One natural question to ask at this point is whether German adjustment patterns were greatly altered by the new employment regulations adopted at the beginning of the 1970s, as has been suggested by some observers. Legislation such as the Works Constitution Act is often treated as an exogenous event that forces significant changes in the typical employer's behavior. It may be more realistic, however, to treat such legislation as a codification of what has come to be viewed as best practice. If this view is correct, the Works Constitution Act may have forced changes in the behavior of some marginal employers whose previous behavior lay outside the norm but is unlikely to have caused major changes in the behavior of the typical employer. In that case, we would not expect to find significant differences between labor adjustment during the pre-1973 period and the post-1973 period.

In an effort to address this question, we have fit German models like those reported in table 4-1 and table 4-2 for the 1962–72 period. The earliest year for which we have German data is 1962, and 1972 is the year before the Works Constitution Act took effect. To facilitate comparison between these estimates and those for the 1974–84 period, tables 4-3 and 4-4 present the German estimates for both time periods.

The production employment elasticity estimates in table 4-3 reveal that the initial adjustment of German production employment to changes in shipments was low even before the passage of more restrictive job security legislation in the early 1970s. These findings suggest that it would be a mistake to blame slow German adjustment exclusively on German employment protection laws. At the same time, the findings indicate that, at least in some industries, production employment responded more sluggishly to changes in shipments over the 1974–84

Table 4-3. Production Employment Elasticities, Germany, 1962–72 versus 1974–84

Industry	Current quarter	One quarter	Two quarters	Four quarters	Six quarters
Nonelectrical machinery					
1962–72	0.170**	0.389**	0.542**	0.605	0.564
1974–84	0.052	0.129	0.241	0.482	0.591
Primary metals					
1962–72	0.095	0.265**	0.396**	0.479**	0.529**
1974–84	0.039	0.115	0.170	0.260	0.298
Autos					
1962–72	0.165	0.389**	0.556**	0.816**	0.803
1974–84	0.097	0.241	0.288	0.444	0.553
Stone, clay, and glass					
1962–72	0.106	0.195	0.262	0.285	0.286
1974–84	0.070	0.144	0.216	0.396	0.544
Electrical equipment					
1962–72	0.231	0.543	0.829	1.026	0.919
1974–84	0.188	0.427	0.695	1.084	1.101
Paper					
1962–72	0.188	0.388	0.596	0.864	0.936
1974–84	0.099	0.218	0.348	0.531	0.644
Textiles					
1962–72	0.128	0.345	0.538	0.768	0.668
1974–84	0.056	0.169	0.321	0.629	0.733
Instruments					
1962–72	0.152	0.379	0.546	0.685	0.742
1974–84	0.102	0.239	0.410	0.846	1.002
Leather					
1962–72	0.128	0.330	0.534	0.532	0.269**
1974–84	0.112	0.288	0.470	0.724	0.704
Apparel					
1962–72	0.084	0.282	0.510	0.588**	0.297**
1974–84	0.092	0.264	0.469	0.878	1.016
Printing					
1962–72	0.099	0.248	0.354	0.467*	0.483**
1974–84	0.132	0.335	0.439	0.705	0.985

**1962–72/1974–84 difference significant at 0.05 level, two-tailed test.
*1962–72/1974–84 difference significant at 0.10 level, two-tailed test.

Table 4-4. *Production Hours Elasticities, Germany, 1962–72 versus 1974–84*

Industry	Current quarter	One quarter	Two quarters	Four quarters	Six quarters
Nonelectrical machinery					
1962–72	0.187	0.453	0.611	0.684	0.604
1974–84	0.119	0.274	0.373	0.463	0.455
Primary metals					
1962–72	0.271*	0.517	0.546	0.659	0.596
1974–84	0.443	0.466	0.441	0.589	0.552
Autos					
1962–72	0.552	0.849**	0.996**	1.137**	1.036
1974–84	0.451	0.568	0.634	0.730	0.808
Stone, clay, and glass					
1962–72	0.234	0.326	0.336	0.315	0.287
1974–84	0.280	0.372	0.470	0.510	0.619
Electrical equipment					
1962–72	0.318**	0.717	0.996	1.101	0.839
1974–84	0.733	0.811	0.982	1.207	0.939
Paper					
1962–72	0.456	0.634*	0.653	0.875	0.722
1974–84	0.265	0.297	0.385	0.409	0.390
Textiles					
1962–72	0.412	0.524	0.715	0.841	0.584
1974–84	0.402	0.397	0.440	0.754	0.726
Instruments					
1962–72	0.380	0.679	0.720	0.948	0.962
1974–84	0.280	0.284	0.381	0.852	0.712
Leather					
1962–72	0.299	0.640	0.796	0.425**	−0.097**
1974–84	0.342	0.561	0.627	0.826	0.659
Apparel					
1962–72	0.207	0.283	0.492	0.488**	0.079**
1974–84	0.341	0.504	0.543	1.022	0.916
Printing					
1962–72	0.146**	0.353	0.386	0.328	0.174**
1974–84	0.447	0.438	0.329	0.482	0.784

** 1962–72/1974–84 difference significant at 0.05 level, two-tailed test.
* 1962–72/1974–84 difference significant at 0.10 level, two tailed test.

period than it had during the 1962–72 period. The point estimate of current-quarter adjustment as well as adjustment over one and two quarters declined in most industries, though only in the nonelectrical machinery, primary metals, and automobile industries are any of these pre-1973 versus post-1973 differences statistically significant. Over four to six quarters, however, no consistent pattern of reduced adjustment in the post-1973 period emerges, and in several cases there is evidence of an increase in employment adjustment over those horizons.

Consistent with the long history of short-time compensation in Germany, comparison of table 4-4 with table 4-3 reveals much greater initial adjustment of production worker hours than of production worker employment even before the introduction of strengthened job security regulations in 1973. Because production hours is the product of employment and average hours per worker, this fact implies that in both periods the adjustment of average hours per worker accounts for most of the short-run adjustment of total hours in Germany. Whereas the results in table 4-3 suggest that employment adjustment has become somewhat more sluggish, the results in table 4-4 suggest that the adjustment of total hours has not slowed. In several industries (primary metals, electrical equipment, and printing), the contemporaneous response of hours to a change in shipments is significantly larger in the 1974–84 period than in the 1962–72 period. These findings reflect a greater adjustment of average hours per worker in the later period and are consistent with the fact that the use of short time became less restrictive while employment protection laws became more restrictive between the two periods. Only in the automobile and paper industries is there evidence of a significant slowing in total adjustment of hours.[8]

Despite these differences in adjustment over two periods, the main message of the results reported in tables 4-3 and 4-4 is that adjustment in the two periods was extremely similar. Even in the earlier period, German firms adjusted employment levels very little in the short run to changes in demand, instead relying primarily on the adjustment of average hours per worker.

One might argue that differences in the demand conditions that prevailed during the 1962–72 and 1974–84 periods would have led one to expect greater adjustment during the later period had tightened regulations not prevented it. Like many European countries, Germany

8. Comparable models estimated for the United States show no consistent pattern of change in either employment or hours adjustment.

strengthened employment protection laws in the late 1960s and early 1970s, on the eve of the 1973–74 oil price shock and subsequent recession. Several commentators have asserted that, while compliance with these laws would have been fairly easy had the stable, high-growth economic conditions that characterized the 1960s persisted, the new laws severely hampered industrial adjustment in the volatile and slow-growth environment that characterized the post-1973 period.

This widely held view, however, is not entirely consistent with the facts for Germany. First, it is not generally true that industry demand was more volatile in the post-1973 period. In most of the eleven industries that we have studied, the cyclicality of shipments (as measured by the standard deviation of the logarithm of shipments around trend) was roughly the same over the 1962–72 period as over the 1974–84 period, and in only one case (paper) were shipments more volatile over the later period. German manufacturing experienced a recession during the 1960s, and even without the more stringent regulations on layoffs introduced later, little short-run adjustment of employment occurred.

It is true that in certain industries, notably primary metals, textiles, and apparel, German producers have had to cope with a steady trend decline in shipments during the post-1973 period. However, in all of the industries we have examined including these three, productivity growth was much greater in Germany than in the United States during the 1974–84 period. Although many factors affect productivity growth, these trends support the argument that German employment protection laws did not, in general, seriously hamper longer-term restructuring in German manufacturing.

Sensitivity Analysis

One potential concern about the estimates we have reported is whether our findings are sensitive to the precise estimating equation used. We have experimented with a number of specifications.[9] While the appropriate interpretation of the results reported can be debated, the results themselves are quite robust.

9. These specifications include using monthly rather than quarterly observations; using a first-difference rather than a levels specification; adding the seventh lag of the dependent variable as an explanatory variable, to capture any effects of initial conditions on current labor input; and adding more lagged shipments terms on the right hand side. We have also estimated rational expectations models that assume quadratic adjustment costs, specified as described in appendix A.

Another issue concerns the comparability of the German and U.S. data on hours. Whereas the German data measure hours actually worked, the U.S. data measure hours paid for, including time spent on vacation and other sorts of paid leave. The distinction between actual and paid hours will affect estimated elasticities if, for example, employers are able to schedule vacation time during slack periods.[10] Wholly comparable series are not available for the two countries. Some information on actual weekly hours and paid weekly hours, however, was collected and reported for selected German manufacturing industries in January, April, July, and October of each year from 1964 through 1972. Our analysis of these data reveals no consistent difference in employers' ability to adjust actual versus paid hours of work, though the estimates obtained were imprecise.[11] In addition, we have estimated similar models for other time periods. None of our conclusions is sensitive to the time period selected.

The Behavior of Shipments

In our view, the major question about the results just reported is whether our qualitative conclusions on German versus U.S. employment and hours adjustment would have been different had the demand conditions facing employers in the two countries over the 1974–84 period been more similar. As a first step in addressing this issue, we turn now to a more systematic examination of differences in the characteristics of the shipments time series for comparably defined German and U.S. industries.

Table 4-5 summarizes some key aspects of the shipments series over the 1974–84 period for our matched German and U.S. industries. The first column reports a measure of the persistence of shocks to shipments; the second reports a measure of the cyclicality of shipments around trend; and the third presents the average annual growth rate of shipments. Our methodology for calculating these measures of the persistence, cyclicality and trend growth of shipments is discussed in appendix A.

10. The data we use are seasonally adjusted and thus regularly scheduled holidays during seasonally slack periods should not be a concern.
11. These results are available upon request. The survey from which these data were obtained has been continued, but the questions about actual hours worked were dropped after 1972.

Table 4-5. *Behavior of Shipments, 1974–84*

Industry	Persistence[a]	Cyclicality[a]	Trend[a]
Nonelectrical machinery			
Germany	0.255	0.037	0.016
United States	0.919	0.071	0.015
Primary metals			
Germany	0.842	0.064	−0.022
United States	0.848	0.124	−0.032
Autos			
Germany	0.704	0.059	0.049
United States	0.908	0.200	0.005
Stone, clay, and glass			
Germany	0.554	0.056	−0.005
United States	0.910	0.078	0.000
Electrical equipment			
Germany	0.684	0.037	0.020
United States	0.815	0.066	0.034
Paper			
Germany	0.581	0.042	0.017
United States	0.920	0.056	0.012
Textiles			
Germany	0.785	0.038	−0.023
United States	0.888	0.087	−0.021
Instruments			
Germany	0.779	0.037	0.003
United States	0.794	0.045	0.028
Leather			
Germany	0.444	0.039	0.002
United States	0.679	0.070	−0.035
Apparel			
Germany	0.558	0.033	−0.023
United States	0.868	0.084	−0.014
Printing			
Germany	0.799	0.032	0.028
United States	0.958	0.063	0.031

a. Persistence is defined as the lagged ln(shipments) coefficient from a regression of ln(shipments) on lagged ln(shipments) and time trend terms. Cyclicality is the standard deviation of the residual of a regression of ln(shipments) on time trend terms, and trend is the implied annual growth rate from this regression calculated at the midpoint of the period.

If changes in shipments are highly persistent, a positive shock that raises today's shipments above trend will imply that shipments in subsequent quarters also can be expected to lie above their trend value. We define persistence as the proportional amount by which expectations about the next quarter's shipments should be raised given a one unit shock to this quarter's shipments. [12] Our expectation is that employers should adjust labor less completely when changes in shipments are less persistent. Table 4-5 shows that in most industries shocks to shipments are much less persistent in Germany than in the United States. All else the same, this difference would lead one to expect that German employers would adjust labor input less completely to changes in shipments than would U.S. employers.

The cyclicality of shipments also might affect labor adjustment. Insofar as there are substantial fixed costs associated with mass layoffs or constraints on employers' ability to carry out such layoffs at all, one might expect more complete adjustment to small perturbations in shipments than to large ones. Small downturns may be accommodated through attrition, and small-scale layoffs are subject to less stringent regulation than are mass layoffs. For these reasons, hiring to accommodate a modest upturn might be perceived as less risky than hiring to accommodate a larger increase in shipments. [13] In all of the industries for which we have matched data, German shipments exhibit smaller fluctuations around trend than do U.S. shipments. These differences are consistent with the pattern revealed in figure 4-1, which shows that German industries did not experience the pronounced contraction during the early 1980s borne by U.S. industries.

As was seen in figure 4-1, the shipments series of German and U.S. matched industries for the most part have exhibited similar trends. The only two exceptions to this generalization are the automobile industry, in which German shipments have risen faster than U.S. shipments, and the leather industry, in which German shipments did not experience the serious decline that U.S. shipments did.

12. More precisely, our measure of persistence is the coefficient on the lagged value of the logarithm of shipments from a linear regression of the logarithm of shipments on its own lagged value plus a constant, a time trend, and the square of the time trend.

13. Hamermesh (1989) has argued that, if there are large fixed costs to laying off or hiring workers such that it is only cost effective to adjust the work force in large increments, firms will adjust employment only when demand shocks are large. This argument is most applicable to assembly line technologies, where it generally makes sense to shut down or reopen an entire shift or production line.

A priori, it is not obvious how German employers would have responded to the U.S. demand environment. On the one hand, shocks to shipments are far more persistent in the United States than in Germany. All else the same, one would expect that greater persistence would have led German employers to adjust labor input more completely in response to changes in shipments. On the other hand, U.S. shipments are subject to larger fluctuations around trend than are German shipments. Large fluctuations might well be more difficult for German employers to adjust to, and so they might have adjusted less completely to changes in economic conditions of the magnitude experienced by American producers.

Cross-Industry Variation in Adjustment

The cross-sectional models reported in table 4-6 and table 4-7 represent an effort to quantify the potential importance of these competing forces. The dependent variables in these equations are the estimated current-quarter, two-quarter, and six-quarter responses of production employment and production hours, respectively, to a change in shipments for the most disaggregated set of industries for which data were available in each country (thirty-one industries in Germany and forty-nine industries in the United States). Similar models were fit using the one-quarter and four-quarter employment and hours elasticities as dependent variables. We include measures of the persistence and cyclicality of shipments defined in the same way as those reported in table 4-5 for our eleven matched industries as explanatory variables in these models. Additional control variables were also included. [14]

The results reported in table 4-6 and table 4-7 indicate that, at least in Germany, the characteristics of the time series of shipments in an industry bear the expected relationship to estimated labor adjustment. The results for Germany are of special interest for answering the question of how German employers would have adjusted had they faced conditions like those facing U.S. employers. As predicted, the cross-sectional results suggest that greater persistence of changes in shipments leads to greater adjustment, but that a greater amplitude in the fluctuations of shipments around trend is associated with smaller proportional adjustment.

14. We experimented with the inclusion of a variable capturing trend growth in shipments, but the coefficient on this variable was small, it was never statistically significant, and its inclusion had little effect on the other estimates. For these reasons, it was excluded from the models reported here.

Table 4-6. *Determinants of Production Employment Adjustment*

Item	Mean[a]	Current quarter	Two quarters	Six quarters
		Dependent variable: employment elasticity over[b]		
Germany				
Persistence of *ln*(shipments)	0.648	0.082	0.318	0.404
	[0.213]	(0.068)	(0.147)	(0.245)
Cyclicality of *ln*(shipments)	0.066	−0.323	−1.128	−3.537
	[0.045]	(0.336)	(0.730)	(1.211)
Proportion female in production employment	0.277	0.003	0.230	0.246
	[0.216]	(0.070)	(0.153)	(0.253)
Share of labor costs in value added	0.570	−0.141	0.193	0.369
	[0.154]	(0.095)	(0.206)	(0.341)
R-squared	. . .	0.193	0.324	0.395
United States				
Persistence of *ln*(shipments)	0.793	0.130	−0.024	−0.111
	[0.130]	(0.182)	(0.286)	(0.360)
Cyclicality of *ln*(shipments)	0.087	1.124	1.778	0.441
	[0.039]	(0.663)	(1.044)	(1.314)
Proportion female in production employment	0.290	−0.211	−0.149	−0.515
	[0.205]	(0.109)	(0.171)	(0.215)
Share of labor costs in value added	0.504	0.924	1.588	1.806
	[0.109]	(0.214)	(0.337)	(0.424)
R-squared	. . .	0.471	0.459	0.390

a. The numbers in brackets are standard deviations.
b. The numbers in parentheses are standard errors of the estimates.

We also included the proportion female in production employment and labor's share of value added, each evaluated at the midpoint of the period, as explanatory variables. We expected that the proportion female in production employment might have a positive effect on the estimated production employment elasticity. The female quit rate is higher than the male quit rate, which should make it possible to reduce female employment more quickly without resort to layoffs. Particularly in Germany, we suspect that the average cost of laying off a female worker is lower than that of laying off a male worker. In the German equations, the coefficient on the proportion female variable was positive, though not statistically significant. In the U.S. equations, its sign was actually negative, though generally insignificant.[15]

15. The significant negative coefficients on the percent female variable in the six-quarter response equations are something of a puzzle.

Table 4-7. *Determinants of Production Hours Adjustment*

		Dependent variable: employment elasticity over[b]		
Item	Mean[a]	Current quarter	Two quarters	Six quarters
Germany				
Persistence of *ln*(shipments)	0.648	0.424	0.342	0.528
	[0.213]	(0.141)	(0.195)	(0.249)
Cyclicality of *ln*(shipments)	0.066	−2.113	−2.047	−3.639
	[0.045]	(0.697)	(0.965)	(1.235)
Proportion female in production employment	0.277	−0.081	−0.035	−0.093
	[0.216]	(0.146)	(0.202)	(0.258)
Share of labor costs in value added	0.570	0.298	0.335	0.379
	[0.154]	(0.196)	(0.272)	(0.348)
R-squared	. . .	0.436	0.258	0.361
United States				
Persistence of *ln*(shipments)	0.793	0.376	0.327	0.342
	[0.130]	(0.229)	(0.331)	(0.398)
Cyclicality of *ln*(shipments)	0.087	1.319	1.726	0.188
	[0.039]	(0.837)	(1.207)	(1.452)
Proportion female in production employment	0.290	−0.228	−0.142	−0.499
	[0.205]	(0.137)	(0.198)	(0.238)
Share of labor costs in value added	0.504	1.227	1.977	1.999
	[0.109]	(0.270)	(0.389)	(0.468)
R-squared	. . .	0.500	0.492	0.386

a. The numbers in brackets are standard deviations.
b. The numbers in parentheses are standard errors of the estimates.

The share of labor costs in value added might be expected to have a positive effect on employment and hours elasticities. Labor's share in value added may proxy for elements of the industry's technology, capturing the extent to which labor is a fixed versus a variable input in the production process. If labor's share is small, it might indicate that the amount of labor input required in the production process is relatively insensitive to output levels. In addition, the larger labor's share, the greater the economic incentive management has to reduce labor input when demand falls. Interestingly, the variable measuring labor's share has a large and statistically significant effect on employment and hours elasticities in the United States, but has no significant impact on these elasticities in Germany.

Given the potentially important influence of demand conditions on labor adjustment in German industry, we have used the German coefficients estimated for the persistence and cyclicality variables reported in table 4-6 and table 4-7 to construct "corrected" adjustment estimates for the eleven German industries for which employment and hours estimates were reported in earlier tables. These adjusted numbers represent a rough estimate of how German employers would have varied production employment and total production hours had they faced demand conditions like those faced by U.S. employers. In all eleven industries, our estimate of the responsiveness of German employment and hours to changes in shipments was subject to an upward adjustment reflecting the greater proportional adjustment that would have been expected had German shipments been more persistent and a downward adjustment reflecting the reduced proportional adjustment that would have been expected had German shipments been more cyclical. The original unadjusted numbers first reported in table 4-1 and table 4-2 are reproduced in table 4-8 and table 4-9 alongside the new adjusted numbers.

Making these adjustments in general has little effect on the estimated employment and hours elasticities. In two industries (nonelectrical machinery and stone, clay, and glass), however, the adjusted elasticities are much larger than the original estimates. In both of these industries, the unadjusted German production employment elasticities were significantly less than the U.S. elasticities out to four or six quarters; the unadjusted German hours elasticity estimates for most time horizons were also lower than the U.S. estimates, suggesting that adjustment of average hours per worker in Germany did not fully compensate for the lack of employment adjustment. The results from table 4-8 and table 4-9, however, suggest that a large part of the cross-country differences for these industries can be ascribed to differences in demand conditions in the two countries. In both nonelectrical machinery and stone, clay, and glass, the persistence of the German shipments series is far below the persistence of the U.S. shipments series, while the cross-country difference in the cyclicality of shipments is less marked. Had these two German industries faced demand conditions comparable to those found in the United States, the gaps between the German and U.S. employment and hours elasticities would have been closed or at least greatly reduced.

Only for the primary metals and auto industries do the corrections for differences in demand conditions result in much lower employment and hours elasticities. In both of these industries, U.S. shipments are far more cyclical than German shipments, which leads to a substantial

Table 4-8. *Unadjusted versus Adjusted Production Employment Elasticities, Germany, 1974–84*

Item	Current quarter	One quarter	Two quarters	Four quarters	Six quarters
Nonelectrical machinery					
Unadjusted	0.052	0.129	0.241	0.482	0.591
Adjusted	0.095	0.249	0.413	0.732	0.737
Primary metals					
Unadjusted	0.039	0.115	0.170	0.260	0.298
Adjusted	0.020	0.068	0.104	0.262	0.087
Autos					
Unadjusted	0.097	0.241	0.288	0.444	0.553
Adjusted	0.068	0.174	0.193	0.521	0.136
Stone, clay, and glass					
Unadjusted	0.070	0.144	0.216	0.396	0.544
Adjusted	0.092	0.205	0.303	0.530	0.607
Electrical equipment					
Unadjusted	0.188	0.427	0.695	1.084	1.101
Adjusted	0.189	0.433	0.704	1.133	1.051
Paper					
Unadjusted	0.099	0.218	0.348	0.531	0.644
Adjusted	0.122	0.282	0.440	0.659	0.731
Textiles					
Unadjusted	0.056	0.169	0.321	0.629	0.733
Adjusted	0.049	0.152	0.299	0.668	0.601
Instruments					
Unadjusted	0.102	0.239	0.410	0.846	1.002
Adjusted	0.100	0.236	0.406	0.852	0.982
Leather					
Unadjusted	0.112	0.288	0.470	0.724	0.704
Adjusted	0.122	0.316	0.511	0.812	0.690
Apparel					
Unadjusted	0.092	0.264	0.469	0.878	1.016
Adjusted	0.100	0.291	0.509	0.995	0.959
Printing					
Unadjusted	0.132	0.335	0.439	0.705	0.985
Adjusted	0.135	0.346	0.454	0.765	0.939

downward revision of the estimated German employment and hours elasticities. In both cases, the unadjusted German production employment and hours elasticities were already generally below the corresponding U.S. elasticities. Adjusting the elasticities only widens the gap. We return to the question of how to interpret the unusual adjustment patterns in these two industries below.

Table 4-9. *Unadjusted versus Adjusted Production Hours Elasticities, Germany, 1974–84*

Item	Current quarter	One quarter	Two quarters	Four quarters	Six quarters
Nonelectrical machinery					
Unadjusted	0.119	0.274	0.373	0.463	0.455
Adjusted	0.327	0.414	0.529	0.791	0.680
Primary metals					
Unadjusted	0.443	0.466	0.441	0.589	0.552
Adjusted	0.319	0.333	0.320	0.592	0.336
Autos					
Unadjusted	0.451	0.568	0.634	0.730	0.808
Adjusted	0.239	0.319	0.415	0.831	0.402
Stone, clay, and glass					
Unadjusted	0.280	0.372	0.470	0.510	0.619
Adjusted	0.382	0.438	0.545	0.686	0.724
Electrical equipment					
Unadjusted	0.733	0.811	0.982	1.207	0.939
Adjusted	0.727	0.789	0.968	1.272	0.902
Paper					
Unadjusted	0.265	0.297	0.385	0.409	0.390
Adjusted	0.379	0.377	0.472	0.576	0.519
Textiles					
Unadjusted	0.402	0.397	0.440	0.754	0.726
Adjusted	0.342	0.320	0.375	0.805	0.602
Instruments					
Unadjusted	0.280	0.284	0.381	0.852	0.712
Adjusted	0.271	0.272	0.371	0.859	0.693
Leather					
Unadjusted	0.342	0.561	0.627	0.826	0.659
Adjusted	0.377	0.570	0.644	0.941	0.672
Apparel					
Unadjusted	0.341	0.504	0.543	1.022	0.916
Adjusted	0.364	0.491	0.544	1.175	0.893
Printing					
Unadjusted	0.447	0.438	0.329	0.482	0.784
Adjusted	0.448	0.420	0.319	0.560	0.754

Short-Time Work versus Temporary Layoffs

We have shown that in the German manufacturing sector employers primarily vary the hours that their employees work, rather than the number of employees they hire, in order to adjust labor input to demand changes in the short run. In contrast, American employers extensively

Figure 4-2. *Trends in Short-Time Work in German Industry, 1960–89*

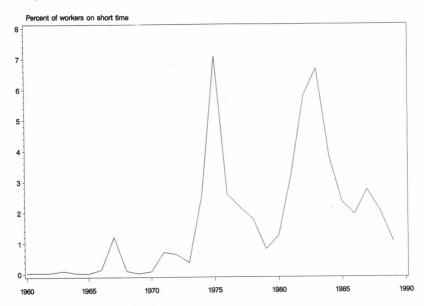

Percent of workers on short time

adjust employment to changes in demand conditions, even in the short run. In Germany unemployment insurance for short-time work is an important component of the unemployment insurance system and facilitates the use of hours adjustment there. Benefits for short-time work are intended primarily—though not exclusively—for workers affected by temporary reductions in demand. Most states in the United States do not offer benefits to workers on short time, and employers frequently make use of temporary layoffs as a response to short-term declines in demand; such temporary layoffs are virtually unknown in Germany. Below we assess the importance of short-time work in Germany and temporary layoffs in the United States to overall labor adjustment in each country and evaluate the relative merits of short-time work versus temporary layoffs.

Figure 4-2 provides some evidence that fluctuations in short time are a significant factor in German adjustment. The figure depicts the percent of workers in German industry on short-time work annually from 1960 to 1989. During good years few workers are on short time. During the recession in 1967 about 1.2 percent of German industrial workers were on short time. During the recessions in 1974 and 1983 that share rose to about 7 percent. Although the recession in the mid-1970s was far more severe than that in the mid-1960s, the recession in the early 1980s was fairly comparable to that in the mid-1960s.[16] This fact suggests that the liberalization of the short-time system during the 1970s and 1980s was an important factor in the far greater use of short-time benefits observed during the more recent slump.

One way to more directly assess the contribution of short-time work to labor adjustment is to examine how total hours of work would have responded to changes in shipments had no workers been placed on short time, assuming that employers' adjustment behavior otherwise remained unchanged. Using data on the number of workers on short-time work by industry and on the percent reduction in hours experienced by those workers, we constructed estimates of the total number of production worker hours for which short-time compensation was paid for nine of the eleven industries in our original analysis; data on number of workers receiving short time were not available over this period for the primary metals and printing industries.[17] Because the data on short time apply to all workers, while the data on hours of work used thus far in our analysis are for production workers, we had to make some assumptions about the distribution of short-time hours between production and nonproduction workers. We used two extreme assumptions to bound our estimates. The first is that short-time hours are distributed between production and nonproduction workers in proportion to their representation in the work force. The second assumption is that only production workers work short time. Additional details concerning our procedures for constructing time series on production workers' short-time hours under both assumptions are provided in appendix A.

Using these series, it is possible to compare actual hours elasticities to those that would have been observed had no employees been placed on short time (and everything else remained the same as in actual fact). The results of carrying out this exercise are summarized in table 4-10. In each case, the "with short time" adjustment of total production hours to changes in shipments is just the actual adjustment we have reported previously. The "without short time" numbers were derived by first

16. Specifically, the peak-to-trough decline in the growth rate of shipments was very similar during the two recessions, though the mid-1960s recession exhibited only one year of negative growth and was followed by a sharper rebound than the downturn of the early 1980s.

17. For primary metals, however, we do know that short time was used extensively. In fact, federal legislation was passed in 1983 to allow steel workers to collect short-time benefits for as long as thirty-six months.

Table 4-10. *Production Hours Elasticities with and without Reductions in Hours Owing to Use of Short Time, Germany, 1974–84*

Item	Current quarter	One quarter	Two quarters	Four quarters	Six quarters
Nonelectrical machinery					
With short time	0.119	0.274	0.373	0.463	0.455
Without short time (1)[a]	0.052	0.117	0.203	0.507	0.705
Without short time (2)[b]	0.011	0.022	0.096	0.505	0.793
Autos					
With short time	0.451	0.568	0.634	0.730	0.808
Without short time (1)[a]	0.239	0.302	0.375	0.523	0.627
Without short time (2)[b]	0.181	0.222	0.294	0.458	0.568
Stone, clay, and glass					
With short time	0.280	0.372	0.470	0.510	0.619
Without short time (1)[a]	0.234	0.271	0.329	0.298	0.557
Without short time (2)[b]	0.222	0.241	0.287	0.232	0.536
Electrical equipment					
With short time	0.733	0.811	0.982	1.207	0.939
Without short time (1)[a]	0.585	0.538	0.588	1.011	0.985
Without short time (2)[b]	0.504	0.364	0.352	0.884	0.988
Paper					
With short time	0.265	0.297	0.385	0.409	0.390
Without short time (1)[a]	0.189	0.185	0.290	0.591	0.633
Without short time (2)[b]	0.166	0.152	0.262	0.645	0.701
Textiles					
With short time	0.402	0.397	0.440	0.754	0.726
Without short time (1)[a]	0.263	0.117	0.057	0.428	0.440
Without short time (2)[b]	0.217	0.027	−0.062	0.324	0.344
Instruments					
With short time	0.280	0.284	0.381	0.852	0.712
Without short time (1)[a]	0.355	0.295	0.128	0.576	0.829
Without short time (2)[b]	0.387	0.294	0.003	0.443	0.875
Leather					
With short time	0.342	0.561	0.627	0.826	0.659
Without short time (1)[a]	0.222	0.311	0.292	0.559	0.459
Without short time (2)[b]	0.196	0.254	0.215	0.496	0.411
Apparel					
With short time	0.341	0.504	0.543	1.022	0.916
Without short time (1)[a]	0.228	0.267	0.222	0.730	0.799
Without short time (2)[b]	0.190	0.207	0.142	0.661	0.763

a. Estimates assume that short-time hours are distributed between production and nonproduction workers according to their proportionate representation in the work force.
b. Estimates assume that production workers account for all short-time hours.

constructing a total production hours series equal to hours worked plus short-time hours, then estimating our standard hours adjustment equation using this variable. The first set of "without short time" numbers is based on the assumption that short-time work is divided between production and nonproduction workers in proportion to their representation in the work force. The second set of "without short time" estimates is based on the assumption that production workers account for all short-time work.

The results reported provide strong evidence that the short-time system plays an important role in German employers' initial adjustment of labor input to changes in output. Assuming that all short time is worked by production workers and excluding instruments, for which our estimates are problematic,[18] the proportion of current quarter adjustment attributable to variation in short-time hours is on average about 45 percent, though this figure varies from as little as 21 percent in stone, clay, and glass to as much as 60 percent in automobiles and over 90 percent in nonelectrical machinery. The proportion of adjustment accounted for by variation in short-time hours at lags of one quarter and two quarters is typically larger, averaging over 60 percent. As would be expected, given that the use of short time generally is intended to be temporary, short time becomes relatively less important at longer horizons, but in some industries accounts for a sizable fraction of total hours adjustment even a year and a half after a shock to shipments.

Several caveats should be attached to the "without short time" numbers reported in table 4-10: the industry definitions used for reporting numbers of workers on short time in most cases are not exactly the same as those used for reporting the employment, hours, and shipments data with which they have been combined; as discussed in appendix A, we have been forced to make some assumptions about the average number of hours of workers on short time; and finally, we have not allowed for quarter-to-quarter changes in the average number of hours on short time for the typical worker collecting short-time benefits, though we believe such changes are of limited importance. Even bearing these caveats in mind, our findings are strongly supportive of the qualitative conclusion that the German short-time system is important in the adjustment of labor input in German manufacturing.

18. The estimates for instruments have the counterintuitive implication that hours worked would have been more responsive to changes in shipments absent the use of short time.

In the United States, the structure of the unemployment insurance system encourages the use of temporary layoffs rather than hours reductions during downturns in demand. Data on temporary layoffs per se are not collected, but labor turnover data collected by the Bureau of Labor Statistics through 1981 enable us to assess the share of layoffs that turn out to be temporary ex post, in the sense that the laid-off individual returns to his or her job. For comparison with our earlier calculations of the share of German total production hours adjustment accounted for by employers' use of short time, we estimate the contribution that temporary layoffs make to the adjustment of production hours in the United States.

Paralleling our analysis of German short time, we construct production hours series for each industry showing what hours would have been had there been no temporary layoffs. Because the turnover data we use to construct these series are for all workers, we must make some assumptions about the distribution of temporary layoffs across production and nonproduction workers. As was done in our analysis of short time for Germany, we make two extreme assumptions to bound our estimates. First, we assume that temporary layoffs are distributed across production and nonproduction workers in proportion to their representation in the work force. Second, and probably closer to the truth, we assume that production workers account for all temporary layoffs. Details concerning our methodology for constructing "without temporary layoff" hours series under both assumptions are provided in appendix A.

Our estimates of hours adjustment with and without temporary layoffs are reported in table 4-11. The "with temporary layoffs" numbers for each industry are essentially the same as the hours elasticities reported in earlier tables, except that they are for a slightly different period than our earlier results. The "without temporary layoffs" numbers for each industry show what adjustment would have looked like had there been no temporary layoffs. The first set of "without temporary layoffs" numbers assumes that temporary layoffs are distributed between production and nonproduction workers in proportion to their representation in the work force. The second set assumes that production workers account for all temporary layoffs.

The results reported in table 4-11 show that temporary layoffs make a large contribution to overall labor adjustment in the U.S. manufacturing sector, though the temporary layoff seems relatively less important as a mechanism of adjustment in the United States than does short-time work in Germany. In the current quarter, temporary layoffs and

Table 4-11. *Production Hours Elasticities with and without Temporary Layoffs and Recalls, United States, 1971–81*

Item	Current quarter	One quarter	Two quarters	Four quarters	Six quarters
Nonelectrical machinery					
With temporary layoffs	0.788	1.173	1.282	1.300	1.466
Without temp. layoffs (1)[a]	0.654	0.966	1.092	1.171	1.352
Without temp. layoffs (2)[b]	0.582	0.853	0.988	1.104	1.293
Primary metals					
With temporary layoffs	0.586	0.678	0.548	0.527	0.530
Without temp. layoffs (1)[a]	0.368	0.382	0.315	0.390	0.392
Without temp. layoffs (2)[b]	0.308	0.300	0.250	0.353	0.352
Autos					
With temporary layoffs	0.770	0.837	0.820	0.787	0.877
Without temp. layoffs (1)[a]	0.635	0.658	0.644	0.622	0.756
Without temp. layoffs (2)[b]	0.587	0.594	0.581	0.561	0.709
Stone, clay, and glass					
With temporary layoffs	0.564	0.839	0.854	1.082	0.990
Without temp. layoffs (1)[a]	0.461	0.612	0.584	0.837	0.831
Without temp. layoffs (2)[b]	0.435	0.554	0.514	0.777	0.789
Electrical equipment					
With temporary layoffs	0.516	0.827	0.975	1.106	0.995
Without temp. layoffs (1)[a]	0.467	0.698	0.834	0.996	0.933
Without temp. layoffs (2)[b]	0.439	0.627	0.759	0.938	0.900
Paper					
With temporary layoffs	0.823	0.993	0.848	0.852	1.180
Without temp. layoffs (1)[a]	0.677	0.778	0.639	0.710	0.984
Without temp. layoffs (2)[b]	0.630	0.709	0.572	0.665	0.921
Textiles					
With temporary layoffs	0.712	0.964	0.671	0.481	0.751
Without temp. layoffs (1)[a]	0.652	0.887	0.627	0.443	0.697
Without temp. layoffs (2)[b]	0.643	0.875	0.620	0.437	0.689
Instruments					
With temporary layoffs	0.507	0.808	0.852	1.114	1.307
Without temp. layoffs (1)[a]	0.461	0.736	0.790	1.065	1.248
Without temp. layoffs (2)[b]	0.433	0.690	0.751	1.035	1.211
Leather					
With temporary layoffs	0.413	0.645	0.568	0.338	0.296
Without temp. layoffs (1)[a]	0.374	0.601	0.522	0.303	0.257
Without temp. layoffs (2)[b]	0.368	0.594	0.514	0.296	0.251
Apparel					
With temporary layoffs	0.226	0.384	0.541	0.284	0.459
Without temp. layoffs (1)[a]	0.193	0.339	0.478	0.249	0.402
Without temp. layoffs (2)[b]	0.187	0.332	0.467	0.244	0.392
Printing					
With temporary layoffs	0.067	0.158	0.263	0.287	0.486
Without temp. layoffs (1)[a]	0.066	0.150	0.247	0.273	0.464
Without temp. layoffs (2)[b]	0.064	0.144	0.234	0.262	0.447

a. Estimates assume that temporary layoffs and recalls are distributed between production and nonproduction workers according to their proportionate representation in the work force.
b. Estimates assume that production workers account for all temporary layoffs and recalls.

recalls on average account for about 20 percent of total production hours adjustment, assuming that all temporary layoffs occur among production workers. This figure ranges from a low of 4 percent in printing to a high of 47 percent in primary metals. In most industries the proportion of total labor adjustment accounted for by temporary layoffs and recalls is about the same or somewhat greater over one and two quarters and diminishes thereafter. As was the case with short time in Germany, however, temporary layoffs in the United States account for a sizable fraction of total labor adjustment over four to six quarters in some industries.

From the employer's perspective, there is a sense in which the use of short time and the use of temporary layoffs are close functional substitutes. Both allow a temporary reduction in labor costs during a period of slack demand. There are, however, important respects in which the two differ. First, a temporary layoff may significantly disrupt the production process. Unless the temporary layoff affects the entire work force, it is likely to require a substantial reorganization of work assignments. If senior employees enjoy bumping rights, laying off even a small number of workers may lead to a large number of job reassignments. When workers are later recalled, productivity may suffer as workers who have been away from the job for an extended period become reacclimated to the work they are doing.

Second, there is a significant risk that employees placed on temporary layoff will not be available for recall. Rough calculations based on findings reported by Lawrence F. Katz and Bruce D. Meyer indicate that, over the duration of a temporary layoff that lasts thirteen weeks, 25 percent of workers on temporary layoff take a new job; over the duration of a twenty-six week temporary layoff, 40 percent of those on layoff take a new job.[19] If workers who had been temporarily laid off do not return, the firm must incur the costs of hiring and training replacement workers. One possible reason why temporary layoffs followed by recalls are relatively less important in overall labor adjustment in the

19. Figure 2 in Katz and Meyer (1990) indicates that the aggregate new job hazard, a measure of the instantaneous probability that an unemployed person will take a new job, is about 0.025, while the results in table 6 suggest that, all else the same, the new job hazard is roughly 40 percent lower for persons who initially expect to be recalled to their previous job. Given that about 75 percent of their sample begins their layoff spell expecting to be recalled, a reasonable guess is that the new job hazard for this group is about 0.021. This is the hazard assumed in arriving at the numbers in the text.

United States than is short-time work in Germany is that many workers on temporary layoff find new work and never return to their original place of employment. The costs associated with hiring and training new employees largely could be avoided if workers were placed on short time instead of on temporary layoff.[20]

Moreover, short time and temporary layoffs are not the same from the employee's perspective. Workers on temporary layoff are likely to face great uncertainty about whether they will ever be recalled. Findings reported by Katz and Meyer indicate that, among laid off workers who initially believe that they will be recalled, only about 70 percent end up returning to their previous employer.[21] This low percentage in part reflects the fact that some workers choose to take new jobs, but also occurs because many workers never receive recall notices. Rough calculations based on Katz and Meyer's econometric analysis of layoff spells suggests that as many as 25 percent of workers who initially believe that their layoff spell will be temporary do not receive a recall notice within a year following the layoff.[22] Workers on temporary layoff who are never recalled experience longer than average unemployment spells, in part because they are less likely to look for new work than workers who are certain their layoff is permanent and in part because potential employers are reluctant to hire someone who may quit if recalled to their previous job. These lengthy spells of unemployment represent a loss of income for the individual workers and a loss of resources to society.

Extensive reliance on layoffs is also less equitable than work sharing, for it concentrates the costs of adjustment on a relatively small number of workers who suffer large losses of income and other job-related benefits. Short-time work arrangements spread the costs of adjustment more evenly across members of the work force.

20. There also would be some voluntary attrition during an extended period of short-time work, but quit rates are typically far below the loss rates from temporary layoff status implied by Katz and Meyer's figures.

21. Katz and Meyer (1990, p. 981).

22. Katz and Meyer's figure 2 indicates that the aggregate recall hazard, a measure of the instantaneous probability that an unemployed person will be recalled to the previous job, averages about 0.050 during the first fifteen weeks following a layoff, then drops to about 0.010. The results in their table 6 suggest that the recall hazard is about ten times greater for persons who initially expect to be recalled than for persons who do not. A reasonable guess is thus that the recall hazard for persons who begin their spell expecting to be recalled is about 0.065 during the first fifteen weeks of a layoff spell and about 0.013 thereafter. These are the hazards used to compute the numbers in the text.

Short-time work may be used to accommodate structural as well as cyclical downturns. In a permanent decline in demand, the use of short-time work does not prevent employment reductions; rather, the temporary use of hours reduction measures can help an employer achieve work force reductions with minimal resort to layoffs. By extending the time over which these work force reductions occur, employers can make greater use of attrition and other alternatives to layoff.

The use of short-time work in instances of structural adjustment is, however, more controversial. Economists typically take the position that in a permanent decline in demand, workers should be reallocated to other sectors as quickly as possible. To achieve this aim, large-scale layoffs, when necessary, have been advocated, on the assumption that dislocated workers will then be forced to find new employment. Several recent studies of displaced workers in the United States show, however, that workers permanently laid off from their jobs often experience long periods of unemployment. Among displaced workers aged 20 to 61 who lost full-time jobs between 1979 and 1981, for example, 31 percent of male blue-collar workers, 38 percent of female blue-collar workers, 14 percent of male white-collar workers, and 28 percent of female white-collar workers experienced more than a year of subsequent joblessness.[23] Only 65 percent of prime-aged full-time workers displaced during 1984 held full-time jobs in January 1986; 8 percent held part-time jobs, 16 percent were unemployed, and 11 percent had withdrawn from the labor force.[24]

By using short-time work as an interim adjustment measure and relying on attrition to reduce the work force, firms can greatly reduce or even avoid layoffs. In this way, job reductions occur among those who have the most attractive outside opportunities or who are best able to relocate, and those who have poor outside opportunities or who are unable to relocate are not thrown out of work.

Conclusion

While there are important differences in the pattern of adjustment to changes in output in Germany compared with the United States, one cannot conclude that German employers are less able to adjust than their

23. Podgursky and Swaim (1987, p. 216).
24. Seitchik and Zornitsky (1989, p. 67).

U.S. counterparts. German companies rely much more on the adjustment of average hours, including the use of short-time work, to reduce labor input during downturns; American companies make greater use of layoffs, including temporary layoffs. At least in the German manufacturing sector, adjustment of hours per worker serves as a short-run substitute for the adjustment of employment levels; in the medium run, the proportional adjustment of German employment to changes in shipments is comparable to that in the United States.

Likely reasons for the very different composition of short-term labor adjustments in the two countries are easy to identify. German employers traditionally have offered even blue-collar workers strong job security, and public policies have reinforced this practice. Employment protection laws discourage the adjustment of employment to changes in the demand for labor that may not prove permanent and make rapid employment adjustment difficult, while the German unemployment insurance system encourages reductions in hours during periods of slack demand. In the United States, in contrast, there are no legal barriers to layoffs, and the unemployment insurance system offers positive incentives to lay workers off rather than reduce their weekly hours. The greater use of short-run hours adjustment by German employers implies greater employment stability in Germany than in the United States in the face of temporary fluctuations in demand. Even when downturns require more permanent reductions in the work force, the extensive use of short-run hours adjustment by German employers means that they can rely more on attrition and other voluntary severance measures, and thereby avoid some worker dislocation.

One might ask whether differences in the way that German and U.S. employers adjust labor input in the short run have any effect on employer costs. On the one hand, a reduction in hours may affect both senior and junior employees, whereas temporary layoffs affect primarily the most junior employees. Particularly if senior workers' higher wages include a pure seniority premium, rather than simply reflecting senior workers' higher productivity, a reduction in hours may produce a greater cost savings than would a temporary layoff that reduced labor input by a comparable amount.[25] In addition, greater reliance on hours reductions

---

25. Medoff and Abraham (1980, 1981) provide some evidence that senior workers are paid more than junior workers performing at a comparable level. Abraham and Medoff's (1985) finding that, in many settings, senior workers are favored in promotions also suggests a reward to seniority.

Table 4-12. *The Effects of Social Plans on Work Force Reductions*
Percent of respondents to an employer survey

Original work force reduction plans	Source of influence	
	Length of negotiations	Outcome of negotiations
Prevented	0.0	0.0
Delayed	19.2	12.5
Reduced	4.0	9.2
Not affected	76.8	78.3
Total	100.0	100.0

Source: Hemmer (1988, p. 46).

compared with layoffs lowers the costs of rehiring and retraining during an upturn, and may improve employee morale, resulting in short- and long-run productivity gains. On the other hand, employers may bear substantially higher fixed costs, including fringe benefit costs such as employer-provided health insurance, if they reduce hours rather than lay off workers. Unfortunately, the lack of complete and comparable data on labor costs prevents us from carrying out a full analysis of this issue.

On the whole, the evidence we have examined suggests that German policies are effective in stabilizing employment in the short run without imposing burdensome costs on employers. One might still be concerned, however, that German policies would inhibit longer-term employment reductions and restructuring when these were needed. Yet, in our analysis we do not find any consistent difference between the medium-run responsiveness of German employment to changes in shipments and that in the corresponding U.S. industry. In some industries, German employment responds less completely over four to six quarters to a change in shipments than does U.S. employment in the same industry; in other industries, the opposite pattern is observed.

Our finding that medium-run German employment adjustment is comparable in magnitude to that in the United States is consistent with responses to several employer surveys that have sought to gauge employers' evaluation of the constraints that job security regulations impose on their behavior. The most recent such survey was that conducted by the Institut der deutschen Wirtschaft, the research arm of the Bundesvereinigung der deutschen Arbeitgeberverbäde. All of the employers in this sample had negotiated a social plan governing compensation to workers affected by a restructuring. As shown in table 4-12, three-quarters of the surveyed employers felt that their restructuring plans had been unaffected by the requirement that they negotiate a social plan, and none felt that attainment of their original work force reduction plans had been prevented. Among the quarter of respondents who felt that their plans had been affected, the most common complaint was that the length of time required for negotiation of a social plan had delayed the implementation of reductions, though about 10 percent of all respondents did say that the outcome of these negotiations led to a scaling back of their original plans for reducing the work force.

Given these findings, one might reasonably ask why the perception that German job security legislation has hampered labor adjustment has been so widespread. The four industries for which our estimates show German employment and hours adjustment to be far below U.S. adjustment even after four to six quarters are nonelectrical equipment, primary metals, automobiles, and stone, clay, and glass. Our analysis suggests that, for the nonelectrical equipment and stone, clay, and glass industries, a large part of the difference in employment and hours elasticities is accounted for by differences in demand conditions in the two countries. This is not true for primary metals or automobiles. Although both of these industries employ a relatively large number of individuals, generalizing from their experience would be misleading.

Still, these exceptions are important and suggest that the effects of providing strong job security for workers may be neither short term nor small. A recent study of restructuring in the steel industry in Germany and other European countries showed that strong job security for workers affected not only employment adjustment in the medium run but also investment and plant closure decisions. More specifically, job security for workers inhibited closure of older facilities and the consolidation of production in more modern, technically efficient plants.[26] Such effects on basic restructuring decisions have potentially important long-run implications.

While adjustment in the German auto industry is also slow by German standards, interestingly, work force adjustment in the American auto industry is becoming more like that in its German counterpart. Recent job security provisions in collective agreements that provide job guarantees, early retirement programs, and job buyout options altered the way American companies adjusted their work forces during the most recent recession. These job security provisions reflect, of course, the

26. Houseman (1991).

strength of the union, the United Auto Workers, and its priorities, and not the effects of U.S. policy.

To a large extent, the same may be true of German industries in which we observe very little employment adjustment. Workers in the primary metals, auto, and nonelectrical equipment industries are represented by the very strong and somewhat radical metal workers' union, IG Metall, which has spearheaded the movement toward shorter work weeks and greater job protection for workers in Germany. The job security provided workers in these industries, however, is atypical of the manufacturing sector and goes well beyond the protection afforded by German law. Therefore, the extent to which very slow adjustment in these industries is the consequence of employment protection laws is highly debatable.

CHAPTER FIVE

The Distributional Effects of Labor Adjustment Policies

C HAPTER 4 EXAMINED the effects that industrial relations practices and public policies have on the adjustment of employment and hours to changes in demand. Whether employers are able to adjust their labor input when demand conditions change is an important determinant of long-run profitability. The way in which employers adjust the work force, in turn, has important implications for how these adjustments are distributed across workers. In the United States, companies rely primarily on hiring and firing to adjust labor input to changing demand. This practice concentrates adjustment on a relatively small number of workers. In Germany, companies rely more heavily on the adjustment of working hours, which allows adjustment to cyclical fluctuations to be distributed more evenly across workers. In addition, practices in the two countries have differing implications for the relative vulnerability of different groups of workers to job loss and joblessness.

Although the average German worker is afforded considerable job security, great variation may occur across workers in the employment protection enjoyed. Under German law, those with low skill levels or short tenures may be especially vulnerable to layoff. For these reasons, youth, women, and foreigners may be at higher risk of job loss than are mature men. The requirement that the selection of workers to be laid off take into consideration social factors such as family dependents may work against youth and women. Discrimination on the basis of individuals' gender or national origin has been alleged by some German observers to make women and foreigners more vulnerable to layoffs than are male German nationals. Finally, government policies allowing older, unemployed workers early entry to the pension rolls may have encouraged companies to lay off workers nearing retirement.

Furthermore, it is not only laid-off workers who suffer during a downturn. New or potential entrants to the labor force who fail to find a job are also hurt. Policies that prevent layoffs will not help these individuals, and the use of hiring freezes in lieu of layoffs may exacerbate the effects of a decline on those who might otherwise have entered employment. This is another reason to believe that German practices may be a source of higher unemployment and lower labor force participation rates among youth and women.

In the United States, although layoffs are common, certain groups of workers are likely to have much stronger job security than others. The prevalence of last-in first-out seniority rules for layoffs implies that senior workers' jobs are far more stable than are junior workers' jobs. One consequence of seniority-based layoff rules is that youth and women, who tend to have less tenure than mature men, are apt to face a higher risk of layoff. Layoffs of nonproduction workers during downturns have been less common than layoffs of production workers. Thus, the focus on production workers in the empirical analysis in chapter 4 overstates the employment instability of U.S. workers overall.

In the following pages we study the implications that German and U.S. industrial relations practices governing work force adjustment have for who bears that adjustment. In particular, we examine the extent to which adjustment is shifted onto certain groups in each country. A question of special interest is whether, and in what respects, German institutions result in a more or less equal distribution of adjustment in society than do U.S. institutions. We begin by studying occupational differences in employment adjustment patterns using data for production versus nonproduction workers in the German and U.S. manufacturing sectors. Next, we examine patterns in employment, unemployment, and labor force participation by age, sex, and nationality in each country.

Employment Adjustment of Production versus Nonproduction Workers

The work load of nonproduction workers in the manufacturing sector tends to be less sensitive to production levels than does the work load of those more directly involved in the production process. For technological reasons, we thus would expect companies in both countries to adjust their production work force proportionately more than their nonproduction work force in response to changing demand conditions.

Because of institutional differences between the two countries, however, we might expect differences in the adjustment of production and non-production employment to be less marked in Germany than in the United States.

In Germany, both white- and blue-collar workers receive some protection against layoff under the country's dismissal laws. At the same time, German management tends to have considerable discretion to reassign both groups of workers across tasks. Although U.S. employers will lay off salaried staff under sufficiently adverse conditions, and there is a growing perception that white-collar jobs have become less secure in recent years, it has been generally understood that management will try to avoid laying off these employees. In exchange, U.S. managers have enjoyed great discretion in the assignments given to their salaried workers. In contrast, U.S. managers tend to have much less flexibility to reassign blue-collar workers across jobs within the firm, particularly in unionized establishments, but they have much more flexibility to lay off these workers.

Comparing the movements of production and nonproduction employment in particular industries across the two countries allows us to assess the effects of each country's industrial relations practices on how the two groups are treated. Table 5-1 and table 5-2 present statistical evidence, based on data for the 1974–84 period, on differences in the adjustment of production and nonproduction workers in eleven manufacturing industries in Germany and the United States, respectively. The tables show the proportional adjustment of production and nonproduction worker employment to changes in shipments over varying time horizons out to six quarters.

As expected, the differences in adjustment between production and nonproduction workers are most striking in the United States. In Germany, there is relatively little short-run adjustment of either production or nonproduction employment in response to changing demand conditions. Few of the estimated German current quarter adjustment elasticities are statistically significant, and even after a quarter the adjustment of production employment is generally not significantly greater than that of nonproduction employment.[1] Only over longer periods does the

1. To determine the statistical significance of the production-nonproduction differences in tables 5-1 and 5-2, we used seemingly unrelated regression techniques to estimate unconstrained and constrained versions of the equations, which permitted us to construct chi-squared statistics for hypothesis testing. The same approach was used to test the significance of the male-female differences in tables 5-7 and 5-8.

Table 5-1. *Production versus Nonproduction Employment Elasticities, Germany, 1974–84*

Industry	Current quarter	One quarter	Two quarters	Four quarters	Six quarters
Nonelectrical machinery					
Production workers	0.052	0.129*	0.241*	0.482*	0.591*
Nonproduction workers	0.026	0.014	0.073	0.209	0.239
Primary metals					
Production workers	0.039	0.115	0.170	0.260*	0.298*
Nonproduction workers	0.106	0.127	0.103	0.069	0.161
Autos					
Production workers	0.097	0.241*	0.288*	0.444*	0.553*
Nonproduction workers	0.057	0.040	−0.037	−0.069	−0.213
Stone, clay, and glass					
Production workers	0.070	0.144	0.216*	0.396*	0.543*
Nonproduction workers	0.094	0.038	0.036	0.125	0.208
Electrical equipment					
Production workers	0.188	0.427*	0.695*	1.084*	1.101*
Nonproduction workers	0.125	0.218	0.312	0.386	0.317
Paper					
Production workers	0.099	0.218	0.348	0.531	0.644
Nonproduction workers	0.096	0.150	0.294	0.431	0.493
Textiles					
Production workers	0.056	0.169	0.321	0.629*	0.733*
Nonproduction workers	0.143	0.222	0.408	0.422	0.418
Instruments					
Production workers	0.102	0.239	0.410	0.846	1.002
Nonproduction workers	0.184	0.268	0.375	0.817	0.925
Leather					
Production workers	0.112*	0.288	0.470	0.724*	0.704*
Nonproduction workers	0.339	0.431	0.496	0.313	0.418
Apparel					
Production workers	0.092	0.264	0.469	0.878	1.016
Nonproduction workers	0.196	0.437	0.585	0.713	0.605
Printing					
Production workers	0.132	0.335	0.439*	0.705*	0.985
Nonproduction workers	0.310	0.242	−0.019	0.059	0.570

Sources: For tables in chapter 5, see appendix C.
*Production/nonproduction difference significant at 0.05 level.

Table 5-2. *Production versus Nonproduction Employment Elasticities, United States, 1974–84*

Industry	Current quarter	One quarter	Two quarters	Four quarters	Six quarters
Nonelectrical machinery					
Production workers	0.633*	0.907*	1.111*	1.104*	1.211*
Nonproduction workers	0.225	0.273	0.330	0.430	0.523
Primary metals					
Production workers	0.410*	0.690*	0.688*	0.763*	0.838*
Nonproduction workers	0.060	0.170	0.216	0.308	0.354
Autos					
Production workers	0.445*	0.597*	0.671*	0.730*	0.699*
Nonproduction workers	0.029	0.086	0.149	0.272	0.299
Stone, clay, and glass					
Production workers	0.260*	0.575*	0.635*	0.764*	0.709*
Nonproduction workers	0.070	0.101	0.159	0.310	0.390
Electrical equipment					
Production workers	0.514*	0.874*	1.022*	0.994	0.916
Nonproduction workers	−0.037	0.085	0.192	0.381	0.427
Paper					
Production workers	0.200	0.395	0.449	0.404	0.535*
Nonproduction workers	0.033	0.100	0.181	0.203	0.219
Textiles					
Production workers	0.197*	0.400*	0.472*	0.317*	0.425*
Nonproduction workers	−0.046	0.003	0.011	0.042	0.021
Instruments					
Production workers	0.263*	0.482*	0.566*	0.651*	0.623
Nonproduction workers	0.039	0.103	0.229	0.404	0.515
Leather					
Production workers	0.203*	0.360*	0.285*	0.201	0.058
Nonproduction workers	−0.065	−0.096	−0.186	−0.145	−0.248
Apparel					
Production workers	0.030	0.157	0.354	0.328	0.338*
Nonproduction workers	−0.082	−0.003	0.186	0.128	0.147
Printing					
Production workers	0.027	0.087	0.125	0.163	0.372*
Nonproduction workers	0.052	0.101	0.135	0.125	0.198

*Production/nonproduction difference significant at 0.05 level.

adjustment of production employment consistently exceed that of non-production employment. In contrast, striking differences between production and nonproduction employment adjustment emerge almost immediately in the United States. In most industries, the response of production employment to a change in shipments is large and rapid, whereas nonproduction employment is initially quite unresponsive to a change in shipments. Many of the short-run employment elasticities estimated for production workers are significantly greater than those estimated for nonproduction workers in the same industry. As in Germany, production employment adjustment over longer periods consistently exceeds nonproduction employment adjustment.

While the adjustment of production employment in the two countries is markedly different, the adjustment of nonproduction employment in Germany and the United States is very similar. In particular, while the short-run adjustment of production employment is typically significantly greater in U.S. industries than in the corresponding German industries, the initial adjustment of nonproduction employment is typically negligible in both countries, so that the two countries' estimated current and one quarter nonproduction employment elasticities are insignificantly different from one another. The personnel practices governing nonproduction workers in the United States have been similar to those that apply to German workers generally. Although experience during the most recent recession suggests that U.S. white-collar workers are becoming more vulnerable to layoff, at least historically nonproduction workers in the United States have enjoyed employment security similar to that enjoyed by German nonproduction workers.

Distributional Effects by Demographic Group

Industrial relations practices may have important implications for the distribution of employment adjustment by demographic group. We use a combination of aggregate and industry data to examine the variability of employment, labor force participation, and unemployment by age and gender. We also look at immigration policy and the extent to which cyclical risk has been shifted onto foreign workers in each country.

The Adjustment of Younger and Older Workers

It is well known that, in the United States, younger workers bear the brunt of adjustment to economic downturns. U.S. companies rely extensively on layoffs, and companies usually select workers for layoff in inverse seniority order. Younger workers, who on average have the least seniority in a company, are thus typically most vulnerable to layoff. In addition, younger workers looking for their first job during a downturn may experience prolonged unemployment or become discouraged and drop out of the labor force for a time.

While the American system of last-in first-out layoffs implicitly provides job security for older, more senior workers and shifts the risk of job loss onto younger, more junior workers, the effects of German public policies and industrial relations practices on the cyclicality of employment by age of worker are less straightforward. In general, German companies rely less on layoffs and more on alternatives, including hiring freezes and attrition, to reduce the work force during downturns than do American companies. Under this system German young people may be less vulnerable to layoffs than American youth, but the Germans also are more likely to be affected by hiring freezes. Although German employment laws provide older workers with strong protection against layoff, older workers may absorb much of the adjustment to adverse demand shocks through early retirement schemes.

There is a common perception that German young people have been insulated from demand fluctuations relative to youth in the United States and in many other European countries, while older workers have absorbed a substantial portion of the employment losses, especially in the 1980s, through government-subsidized early retirement programs. If a particular group bears a disproportionate amount of employment adjustment to demand changes, then, all else the same, the unemployment and labor force participation rates of that group should be relatively more variable. For that reason, we begin our analysis by looking at basic trends in the unemployment rates and labor force participation rates of younger and older workers in the two countries in recent years.

One caveat to be attached to our use of aggregate data to draw inferences about employers' treatment of older compared with younger workers is that, in both Germany and the United States, there is some tendency for workers of different ages to be employed in different sectors. These differences are, however, relatively minor,[2] and consequently it is

2. German Mikrozensus data for 1978 (Statistisches Bundesamt, 1978, p. 47) show no consistent age-group pattern in the share of workers employed in manufacturing, mining, and construction; these sectors accounted for 48 percent of employed 15- to 20-year-olds, 39 percent of those aged 20 to 25, 44 percent of those aged 25 to 35, 48 percent of those aged 35 to 45, 47 percent of those aged 45 to 55, and 42 percent of 55- to 60-year-olds. Age-group differences in the share of workers employed in trade were even smaller. Calculations using U.S. Current Population Survey data for March

reasonable to interpret differences in the behavior of unemployment and labor force participation rates by age group within each country as primarily reflecting differences in the treatment afforded to workers of different ages rather than to differences in their distribution across sectors.

Table 5-3 presents unemployment rates broken out for various age groups for Germany and the United States over the 1974–89 period.[3] One striking difference between the German and the U.S. numbers is the much smaller dispersion of unemployment rates across age groups in Germany than in the United States. In 1983, the difference between the teenage unemployment rate and the unemployment rate for workers aged 55–59 in Germany was 8.7 percentage points; by 1989 the official unemployment rate of workers aged 55–59 was higher than that of teenagers. In the United States, the unemployment rate is the greatest among younger workers and drops abruptly with age. In 1982, for example, the unemployment rate was 23.2 percent for teenagers and 5.6 percent for workers aged 55–59, more than a 17 percentage point differential. Although the unemployment rate of teenagers fell more than that of older workers in subsequent years, the differential was still over 11 percentage points in 1989.

The German apprenticeship system has been widely credited with smoothing the transition between school and work and thereby reducing teenage unemployment. Interestingly, whereas the U.S. unemployment rate for persons aged 20–24 is much lower than that for U.S. teens, the unemployment rate differentials between teenagers and persons in their

---

1976 show that mining, construction, and manufacturing accounted for only 17 percent of employed 15- to 19-year-olds but accounted for between 29 and 33 percent of employed workers in all older age groups, excluding persons over age 65. Trade accounted for 41 percent of employment among those aged 15 to 19 but accounted for 24 percent of employment among those aged 20 to 24 and between 17 and 19 percent of employment of those in all older age groups, again excluding persons over age 65.

3. The German unemployment rates reported in this table and the German labor force participation rates in table 5-4 are statistics based on the Mikrozensus. Data from the same source were used to estimate the models that underlie table 5-5. No wholly comparable by-age-group series are available for Germany and the United States. By-age-group data for Germany based on concepts closer to U.S. concepts are available from Eurostat for selected years. Our comparison of the Mikrozensus data against the Eurostat data indicates that comparisons of unemployment and labor force participation rates across age groups in Germany should be little affected by the use of Mikrozensus rather than Current Population Survey concepts. See appendix C for further details on the Mikrozensus and the Current Population Survey data.

Table 5-3. *Trends in Unemployment Rates by Age Group, 1974–89*
Percent of labor force

Year	15–19[a]	20–24	45–49	50–54	55–59	60–64	15+[a]
			Germany				
1974	2.3	1.8	1.1	1.1	1.4	1.1	1.4
1975	6.6	4.7	2.4	2.1	2.6	2.5	3.4
1976	7.0	5.1	2.7	2.6	3.4	2.9	3.5
1977	6.8	5.3	2.6	2.8	3.1	3.1	3.6
1978	6.4	4.8	2.4	2.6	3.4	2.8	3.5
1979	5.3	3.9	2.2	2.2	3.6	3.0	3.1
1980	4.9	3.5	1.9	2.0	3.1	3.5	2.8
1981	6.0	5.1	2.6	2.7	3.9	3.9	3.7
1982	9.0	8.2	3.7	3.9	5.2	5.1	5.5
1983	14.1	10.6	4.8	4.9	5.4	4.7	7.3
1984	14.2	10.5	5.1	5.8	6.2	3.5	7.7
1985	12.8	10.7	6.0	6.1	8.5	4.8	8.2
1986	10.4	9.0	6.0	6.4	9.0	5.9	7.8
1987	10.2	9.3	6.3	6.7	9.8	6.2	8.0
1988	9.3	8.4	5.9	6.6	11.5	7.7	7.8
1989	8.0	6.7	5.8	6.1	11.7	7.4	7.2
			United States				
1974	16.0	9.1	3.1	2.8	2.8	2.9	5.7
1975	19.9	13.6	5.2	5.2	4.5	4.7	8.7
1976	19.0	12.0	4.5	4.4	4.4	4.6	7.9
1977	17.8	11.0	3.9	4.0	3.7	4.2	7.1
1978	16.4	9.6	3.3	3.3	2.9	2.9	6.1
1979	16.1	9.1	3.1	3.3	2.9	2.9	6.0
1980	17.8	11.5	4.3	3.7	3.3	3.3	7.7
1981	19.6	12.3	4.5	3.9	3.8	3.6	8.2
1982	23.2	14.9	5.7	5.7	5.6	4.9	10.6
1983	22.4	14.5	6.2	6.1	5.8	5.5	10.6
1984	18.9	11.5	5.2	4.5	4.8	4.6	8.1
1985	18.6	11.1	4.8	4.5	4.5	4.0	7.6
1986	18.3	10.7	4.4	4.5	4.3	3.9	7.5
1987	16.9	9.7	4.0	4.0	3.5	3.4	6.8
1988	15.3	8.7	3.6	3.3	3.2	3.1	6.0
1989	15.0	8.6	3.3	3.1	3.3	3.0	5.7

Sources: The German data come from the Mikrozensus and are published by the Statistiches Bundesamt. The U.S. data come from the Current Population Survey and are published by the Bureau of Labor Statistics.
a. For the United States the age brackets are 16–19 and 16+.

early twenties are relatively small in Germany. This pattern is consistent with allegations that the apprenticeship system shifts some unemployment from teenagers onto workers in their early twenties who are making the transition from apprenticeship to regular employment.[4] The differential in unemployment rates between youth aged 20–24 and older workers is, however, still much smaller in Germany than in the United States.

It is also interesting that the unemployment rate in Germany typically increases for the age group 55–59 and then falls off again for workers aged 60 and over. One factor contributing to the high unemployment rate of older workers has been the length of the spells of unemployment they experience. In 1988, about 57 percent (58 percent) of workers aged 55–59 (60–64) who were collecting unemployment benefits had been unemployed for one year or more. In comparison, only about 33 percent of all persons collecting unemployment benefits had been unemployed for one year or more.[5] Older workers who lose their jobs and who want to work often have difficulty finding new employment.

The bulge in the unemployment rate of workers aged 55–59 evident in recent years reflects not only unemployment problems for this age group, but also the de facto early retirement of many in their late fifties in Germany. During the 1980s, such early retirements were facilitated by the changes to the unemployment insurance and social security laws described in chapter 2. Many companies used these programs to help finance early retirement programs by "firing" older workers, who could then collect unemployment benefits for as long as thirty-two months and begin collecting a state pension at age 60.

Fluctuations in employment affect not only unemployment rates but also labor force participation rates. During a downturn, we would expect that some individuals would drop out of the labor force, dampening the rise in unemployment. Conversely, during an upturn, we would expect that more individuals would be enticed into the labor market by better employment prospects, mitigating the fall in unemployment. To analyze how adjustment to demand changes is distributed across workers we must consider the effects of demand changes not only on unemployment but also on labor force participation for each group.

---

4. Casey (1986, pp. 73–74) is among those who argue that some unemployment is shifted from teenagers onto workers in their early twenties.

5. Bundesanstalt für Arbeit (1991, p. 760).

Table 5-4. *Trends in Labor Force Participation Rates by Age Group,*
1974–89
Percent of population

| | Germany | | | | United States | | | |
Year	15–19	20–24	55–59	60–64	16–19	20–24	55–59	60–64
1974	55.2	74.8	57.3	35.9	54.8	74.0	65.6	49.5
1975	54.0	74.2	57.7	33.7	54.0	73.9	65.3	48.4
1976	50.4	74.5	57.7	30.0	54.5	74.7	65.0	47.4
1977	48.1	75.2	58.7	27.6	56.0	75.7	64.8	46.9
1978	47.5	75.5	57.6	24.7	57.8	76.8	64.9	46.6
1979	49.2	75.3	56.4	22.7	57.9	77.5	64.7	47.0
1980	45.0	76.7	56.9	25.6	56.7	77.2	64.4	46.3
1981	43.5	76.4	57.0	26.0	55.4	77.3	64.6	44.8
1982	42.7	76.3	58.1	25.6	54.1	77.1	64.8	44.4
1983	42.5	75.5	58.4	23.8	53.5	77.2	63.8	44.5
1984	43.8	75.5	58.6	21.2	53.9	77.6	64.2	43.8
1985	45.0	77.1	57.5	19.8	54.5	78.2	64.2	43.8
1986	43.7	77.7	58.8	20.3	54.7	78.9	64.5	43.3
1987	42.8	78.4	60.0	21.1	54.7	78.9	65.3	43.3
1988	42.5	78.5	60.4	21.5	55.3	78.7	65.7	43.4
1989	40.8	77.0	59.9	21.5	55.9	78.7	66.6	44.5

Sources: The German data come from the Mikrozensus and are published by the Statistiches Bundesamt. The U.S. data come from the Current Population Survey and are published by the Bureau of Labor Statistics.

Table 5-4 displays basic trends in labor force participation for younger and older workers in Germany and the United States during the 1970s and 1980s. The cross-country differences in labor force participation trends are most striking for teenagers and for older workers aged 60–64. In Germany, the labor force participation rate of persons aged 15–19 dropped sharply, falling from 55.2 percent in 1974 to 40.8 percent in 1989. In contrast, in the United States the labor force participation rate of teenagers displays little trend over time.

In discussing table 5-3 we suggested that the relatively high unemployment rates of German workers aged 55–59 that developed in the 1980s partly reflected the extensive use of early retirement by companies to shed excess labor. Many of these workers collected unemployment insurance while they were in their late fifties, and became officially retired when they reached age 60. While the effects of the early retirement programs should show up in high unemployment rates for workers in their late fifties, they should show up in low labor force participation rates for workers in their early sixties. In Germany, the labor force participation rate of people aged 60–64 plummeted during the 1970s and 1980s, falling from 35.9 percent to 21.5 percent between 1974 and

1989. In the United States, it dropped by only about 5 percentage points over the same period. The dramatic drop in labor force participation of both German teenagers and older individuals reflects, for teenagers, prolonged schooling and, for older workers, the extensive use of early retirement during a period of generally weak economic conditions.

To more formally analyze the distributional effects of demand shocks, we constructed measures of the cyclicality of employment, unemployment, and labor force participation, by age group. The relation between shifts in employment, unemployment, and labor force participation can be seen in the following identity:

(5-1)
$$(E/P)_i = (E/L)_i(L/P)_i \text{ and}$$
$$d\ln(E/P)_i = d\ln(E/L)_i + d\ln(L/P)_i \, ,$$

where E is employment, P is population, and L is the labor force for group i. Note that the employment rate, E/L, is simply equal to one minus the unemployment rate. The identity in equation 5-1 implies that a decrease in group i's employment-to-population ratio may be decomposed into the part due to a change in the unemployment rate and the part due to a change in the labor force participation rate.

To measure the responsiveness of the employment-to-population ratio and its components to output fluctuations by age and sex group, we estimated the following equations:

(5-2)
$$d\ln(E/P)_{it} = \alpha_i + \beta_{1i}g_t + \beta_{2i}g_{t-1} + \epsilon_{it}$$

(5-3)
$$d\ln(E/L)_{it} = \alpha'_i + \beta'_{1i}g_t + \beta'_{2i}g_{t-1} + \epsilon'_{it}$$

(5-4)
$$d\ln(L/P)_{it} = \alpha''_i + \beta''_{1i}g_t + \beta''_{2i}g_{t-1} + \epsilon''_{it},$$

where g is the growth rate of output, the αs and βs are coefficients to be estimated, and the ϵs are error terms. We corrected for first-order serial correlation in the error terms of each equation.

Our measure of output change, g, is the growth rate of gross national product (GNP) for the United States and the growth rate of gross domestic product (GDP) for Germany. The sum of the β_1 and β_2 coefficients in each equation is our measure of the cyclical responsiveness of the dependent variable. Note that $\beta'_1 + \beta'_2 + \beta''_1 + \beta''_2$ is approximately equal to $\beta_1 + \beta_2$.[6] The β' coefficients in equation 5-3 show

6. This identity holds only approximately, rather than exactly, because we allow differences in the serial correlation of the error terms across the three estimating equations.

the contribution of changes in the employment rate (or, equivalently, changes in the unemployment rate) to changes in the employment-to-population ratio; the β'' coefficients in equation 5-4 show the contribution of changes in the labor force participation rate to changes in the employment-to-population ratio. In these equations, any smooth trend growth in the employment-to-population ratio, the employment rate, or the labor force participation rate due to supply-side factors will be captured in the constant term.[7] We use annual data for the 1965–89 period for Germany and the United States to estimate these equations.

Table 5-5 reports these measures of the cyclical response of the employment-to-population ratio, the employment rate, and the labor force participation rate by age for Germany and the United States. As expected, our measure of the cyclicality of the employment-to-population ratio declines steadily with age in the United States, implying that younger people bear a disproportionate amount of employment adjustment. Changes in the labor force participation rate account for a relatively greater proportion of changes in the employment-to-population ratio for teens than for older workers in the United States. Thus, movements in the unemployment rate by age group alone understate the extent to which youth bears the brunt of adjustment in the United States.

The relation of employment cyclicality to age is much less clear-cut in Germany than in the United States. Except for teenagers, the cyclicality of the employment-to-population ratio generally declines with age until age 60, though the differentials in employment adjustment across these age groups are much less pronounced in Germany than in the United States. The shifting of employment adjustment onto younger workers that occurs in the United States does not appear to take place in Germany to nearly the same degree.

One might be tempted to conclude that German teenagers bear less adjustment to demand shocks than do German workers in their twenties. However, for the age group 15–19, the standard error on our measure of the cyclicality of the employment-to-population ratio is so large that we cannot conclude anything definite about the relative size of the

7. The equations we have estimated can be thought of as first-difference versions of models in which the logarithms of E/P, E/L or L/P, in turn, are regressed on a constant, a linear time trend, and the current plus the first lagged value of the logarithm of output. Differencing yields the model specified in the text, with the α parameters equal to the time trend coefficients from the original equations. This methodology is similar to that used in Clark and Summers (1981).

Table 5-5. *Cyclical Response of Employment, Unemployment, and Labor Force Participation by Age Group, 1965–89*[a]

Age	Germany			United States		
	Employ./pop. ratio	Employment rate	Participation rate	Employ./pop. ratio	Employment rate	Participation rate
15–19[b]	0.430	0.797	−0.388	1.789	0.989	0.818
	(0.517)	(0.225)	(0.415)	(0.167)	(0.096)	(0.163)
20–24	0.616	0.530	0.057	0.956	0.810	0.224
	(0.203)	(0.136)	(0.133)	(0.123)	(0.089)	(0.091)
25–29	0.499	0.398	0.101	0.675	0.592	0.094
	(0.164)	(0.088)	(0.100)	(0.084)	(0.060)	(0.065)
30–34	0.553	0.381	0.166	0.542	0.476	0.073
	(0.130)	(0.080)	(0.087)	(0.079)	(0.042)	(0.070)
35–39	0.408	0.299	0.112	0.503	0.435	0.100
	(0.093)	(0.054)	(0.070)	(0.080)	(0.035)	(0.061)
40–44	0.587	0.277	0.270	0.379	0.380	−0.018
	(0.062)	(0.055)	(0.057)	(0.065)	(0.031)	(0.044)
45–49	0.295	0.248	0.049	0.372	0.346	0.004
	(0.076)	(0.046)	(0.058)	(0.089)	(0.033)	(0.064)
50–54	0.349	0.220	0.066	0.520	0.357	0.115
	(0.123)	(0.041)	(0.093)	(0.098)	(0.037)	(0.052)
55–59	−0.040	0.252	−0.278	0.414	0.340	0.085
	(0.161)	(0.082)	(0.143)	(0.101)	(0.029)	(0.091)
60–64	0.475	0.230	0.195	0.334	0.353	−0.048
	(0.734)	(0.087)	(0.754)	(0.188)	(0.036)	(0.194)
65+	0.235	0.021	0.211	0.019	0.217	−0.219
	(0.662)	(0.038)	(0.658)	(0.286)	(0.053)	(0.285)
15+[b]	0.486	0.371	0.068	0.640	0.506	0.138
	(0.092)	(0.064)	(0.097)	(0.073)	(0.050)	(0.033)

a. Standard errors of the estimates are reported in parentheses.
b. For the United States the age brackets are 16–20 and 16+.

adjustment borne by this group. Interestingly, however, unlike the situation in the United States, in Germany the labor force participation rates of younger workers are insensitive to demand conditions. Thus, the sharp drop in labor force participation among German youth shown in table 5-4 seems to be a secular, not a cyclical, phenomenon.

We had speculated that some of the adjustment to demand shocks in Germany would be shifted onto older workers through early retirement programs. At first blush the evidence in table 5-5 would seem to bear this out. The measure of the cyclicality of the employment-to-population ratio increases dramatically for the age group 60–65; this substantial increase occurs because of the sizable responsiveness of the labor force participation rate to demand conditions for workers in this age bracket. However, as was true for teenagers, the standard errors on our estimates of the responsiveness of employment, unemployment, and labor force participation are quite large, and we cannot say anything precise about the extent to which older workers absorb demand shocks in Germany.

Male versus Female Adjustment

The risk of job loss and unemployment may vary between men and women. Both in Germany and in the United States, there are reasons to expect that women might be more vulnerable to layoff than are their male coworkers.

One might expect German women to be more likely to be laid off simply because they are disproportionately employed in less-skilled positions and because they have shorter average tenures than their male coworkers. Skilled workers are more costly to recruit and train, so that employers are less likely to lay them off during downturns that they perceive as temporary. Besides recruitment and training costs, severance costs are an important consideration for German employers in determining whether to lay off a worker. In a collective dismissal, employers must negotiate a social plan with the works council stipulating compensation for affected workers. Compensation measured in weeks of pay typically increases with the worker's skill and tenure. Because women's skill level and tenure are, on average, less than men's, we would expect them to receive proportionately lower compensation in a social plan.

To our knowledge, no data on settlements in social plans broken out by sex exist. The findings from the survey of social plans negotiated between 1980 and 1985 conducted by the Institut der deutschen Wirtschaft include breakdowns for several manufacturing industries.[8] According to the survey, the median social plan settlement in the textile industry, which employs predominantly females in low-skilled jobs, was roughly nine weeks' pay. This compares with a median settlement of roughly sixteen weeks' pay in the metal industry and roughly twenty-nine weeks' pay in the chemical industry, both of which employ pri-

8. The results of this survey are reported in Hemmer (1988).

marily males in higher-skilled positions.[9] These figures are suggestive of differences in settlements by sex.

Advance notice requirements impose an indirect cost that increases with a worker's tenure. Because women have shorter average tenure than men, they are entitled, on average, to shorter notice.

German dismissal laws may contribute in other ways to making women more vulnerable than men to layoff and unemployment. Although in principle these laws apply equally to men and women, they do not apply to individuals with very short tenure or to workers on fixed-term contracts. Women have shorter average tenures and are a bit more likely than men to hold temporary positions other than apprenticeships.[10] More important, some allege that the criteria employers must use in selecting workers to be dismissed in a mass layoff work to the disadvantage of female employees. By law, German employers must consider certain factors, such as the worker's age, length of employment in the company, and responsibility for the support of dependents, in selecting individuals for layoff. A worker may contest his or her dismissal in the labor court on the grounds that these social factors were not taken into account. It is sometimes alleged that, besides being disadvantaged in this process because of their shorter employment tenure, women are disadvantaged in the evaluation of their responsibility for dependent family members. As one German observer wrote, ". . . the two-income argument never works against the employed husband, who is after all the 'head of the family' but only against the wife who 'also' works."[11]

In a similar vein some have suggested that women may be more vulnerable to layoff because they are underrepresented on works councils, which must be consulted on all layoffs and dismissals. In 1984 women constituted about 35 percent of civilian employment in Germany, but they accounted for just 20 percent of all works council representatives.[12]

---

9. To arrive at these estimates, we divided the median severance payment in each industry by the average weekly earnings of blue-collar workers in that industry, as reported for 1984 in Statistisches Bundesamt (1987, pp. 484–86). The median severance payment was 4,783 DM in textiles, 10,726 DM in the metal industry, and 20,083 DM in the chemical industry.

10. Büchtemann and Quack (1989, p. 134).

11. Daübler-Gmelin (1980, p. 341).

12. See Weiss (1987, p. 154). We do not have figures on the proportion of employees in establishments with works councils that are male and female. It is possible that female workers are less likely to work in establishments with works councils, accounting for some of this discrepancy.

While we know of no direct evidence that German women are discriminated against when layoffs occur, there is some evidence that German women believe they are more vulnerable to layoff than their male colleagues. In one question included on a 1984 European Community survey of women in paid employment, women who had male colleagues at work were asked if, in the event of a reduction in force, they thought that men and women would be affected equally, men would be more affected, or women would be more affected.[13] Among the German survey respondents, of those who feared staff cuts (78 percent), 42 percent felt that women were more likely to be affected than their male colleagues, whereas only 5 percent felt that men were more likely to be affected. In response to another question on the major causes of high unemployment among women in their country, 48 percent of German women surveyed identified discrimination by employers as a principal cause of female unemployment. The percent listing discrimination as a major cause of female unemployment was higher in Germany than in any other Community country.[14] German women cited employer discrimination more frequently than any other reason for high female unemployment, including women's inadequate vocational training (42 percent), the decline of industries using female labor (37 percent), and the system of unemployment benefits (28 percent).

Besides being more vulnerable to layoff, women, as a group, may be at greater risk during downturns because they are more likely than men to be entering or reentering the work force and trying to find a job. In particular, women are more likely to interrupt their careers when they marry or have children. Women trying to reenter the labor force, much like youth trying to find their first job, are likely to be squeezed when local or national economic conditions worsen; prime-age males, who are better established in their jobs, are less likely to be affected by a reduction in hiring. One might expect these problems to be more serious in Germany, where employers rely more heavily on hiring freezes and attrition to adjust their labor input, than in the United States.

In the United States one might expect women to be more vulnerable to layoff than men because they typically hold less-skilled positions. As already noted, if a downturn is perceived as temporary, employers will have an economic incentive to retain their more skilled workers, who

13. Commission of the European Community (1984, pp. 27–42).
14. The percentage of Italian women feeling that discrimination was a leading cause of female unemployment in their country was also high (47 percent).

are more expensive to recruit and train. Prevailing practices may be such that employers who lay off highly skilled workers, especially salaried workers, are expected to make some severance payment. This might further discourage layoffs of skilled workers. Female employment may be more cyclical than male employment because individuals are selected for layoff primarily on the basis of seniority, and women's average tenure on the job has been shorter than men's. Finally, because they move in and out of the labor force more often than men, women are likely to experience more unemployment searching for work when they reenter the labor force, particularly during a recession.

In both Germany and the United States, then, women are likely to face higher layoff probabilities than men because they tend to hold less-skilled jobs and because they have shorter tenures than men. German women might be relatively more vulnerable to layoff than American women if, as some observers claim, the requirement that social factors be considered in choosing workers for layoff in Germany works against women, and if German women are otherwise discriminated against when layoff decisions are made.

Before formally examining the variability of male and female employment in the United States and Germany, we look at basic trends in aggregate unemployment and labor force participation rates in the two countries. An important factor confounding the interpretation of these aggregate statistics is that men and women are distributed somewhat differently across sectors of the economy, with men more likely than women to be employed in cyclically volatile sectors, particularly manufacturing, mining, and construction.[15] This condition implies that the cyclical behavior of male and female unemployment and labor force participation rates reflects differences in the distribution of men and women across sectors of the economy as well as differences in the way that employers in a particular sector treat members of the two groups. We also have available some sectorally disaggregated data on male and female employment; our analysis of these data is reported later in the chapter.

Figure 5-1 plots trends in male and female unemployment rates in

15. In Germany, 56 percent of men but just 32 percent of women employed outside of agriculture held jobs in these sectors in 1978. See Statistisches Bundesamt (1979, p. 93). In the United States, manufacturing, mining, and construction accounted for 40 percent of male nonagricultural employment but only 18 percent of female nonagricultural employment in the same year. See U.S. Department of Labor (1982, p. 625).

Figure 5-1. *Civilian Unemployment Rates by Sex, 1964–90*

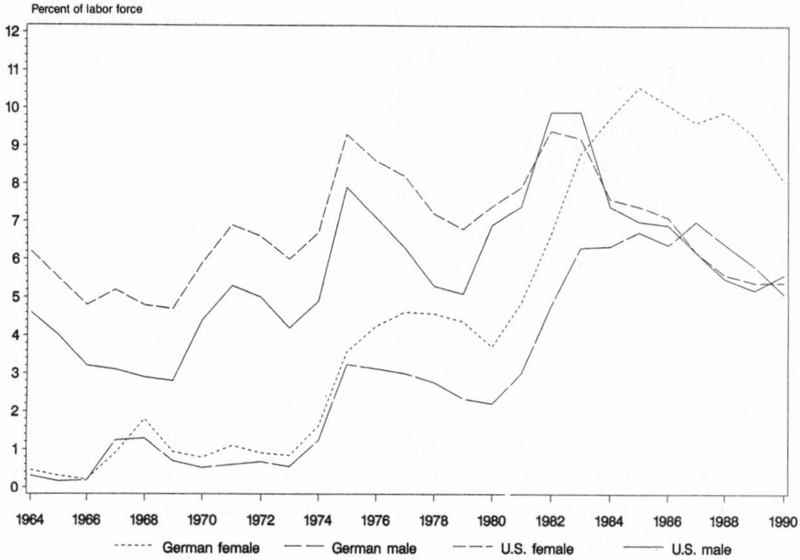

Percent of labor force

Source: For figures in chapter 5, see text and appendix C.

Germany and the United States.[16] Until the mid-1970s, unemployment in Germany was negligible for males and females. The German unemployment rate rose steadily through the 1970s and the first half of the 1980s. The unemployment rate of women rose much more than that of men, however. The total unemployment rate peaked in 1985 at 8.2 percent, but the unemployment rate for males was just 6.7 percent, while that of females was 10.6 percent. A large gap between male and female unemployment rates exists for all age groups. Although these aggregate unemployment figures suggest that women in Germany bore a disproportionate share of adjustment to the slowdown during the 1970s and 1980s, it is difficult to separate out trend from cyclical effects in looking at the raw data. In the United States during the 1960s and 1970s, female unemployment rates were somewhat higher than male

16. The German data used in figures 5-1 and 5-2, and also for the estimation reported in table 5-6, are statistics based on the Mikrozensus. The Bureau of Labor Statistics has produced series on unemployment and labor force participation by sex for Germany adjusted to conform to U.S. definitions. The Bureau of Labor Statistics numbers show a somewhat smaller gap between male and female unemployment rates in Germany than the numbers we report, but similar trends in unemployment and labor force participation for both men and women. Using the Bureau of Labor Statistics data rather than the Mikrozensus numbers to fit the models reported in table 5-6 had no noteworthy effect on the estimated coefficients.

Figure 5-2. *Labor Force Participation Rates by Sex, 1964–90*

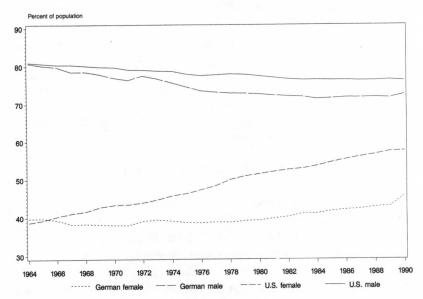

Percent of population

German female   German male   U.S. female   U.S. male

unemployment rates; for most of the 1980s, however, the two rates have been about the same.[17]

Figure 5-2 depicts trends in the labor force participation rate of males and females in Germany and the United States. The labor force participation rate of males in the United States declined slightly over the period, while that of males in Germany declined more sharply, especially in the 1970s and 1980s. The decline in labor force participation among German men primarily captures a decline in labor force participation among teenagers, who are attending school longer, and among older men, who are retiring earlier.

The comparison across countries in female labor force participation trends is even more striking. In Germany, female labor force participation rose slightly over the period, while in the United States it rose dramatically. The relatively small change in Germany reflects the effects of two countervailing forces: among teenage and older women labor force participation was declining, but among prime-aged women (25–55) it was rising. Although cross-country differences in trends in labor force participation rates may be partly because of cultural differences, the trends in Germany suggest that adverse economic conditions during

17. For an analysis of why the gap between male and female unemployment rates in the United States has closed, see Howe (1990).

Table 5-6. Cyclical Response of Employment, Unemployment, and Labor
Force Participation by Sex, 1965–89[a]

Sex	Germany			United States		
	Employ./pop. ratio	Employment rate	Participation rate	Employ./pop. ratio	Employment rate	Participation rate
Males	0.395	0.358	0.017	0.686	0.573	0.107
	(0.098)	(0.062)	(0.074)	(0.071)	(0.049)	(0.029)
Females	0.437	0.370	0.029	0.616	0.425	0.199
	(0.160)	(0.081)	(0.154)	(0.090)	(0.056)	(0.066)

a. Standard errors of the estimates are reported in parentheses.

the 1980s induced both males and females to drop out or stay out of
the labor force.

Table 5-6 presents measures of the sensitivity of male and female
employment to changes in aggregate demand in Germany and the
United States. As was done in table 5-5 for different age groups, table
5-6 breaks down the cyclical response of the employment-to-population
ratio into that part due to changes in the employment rate (one minus
the unemployment rate) and that part due to changes in the labor force
participation rate.

These measures provide little support for the hypothesis that women
absorb a disproportionate amount of adjustment in Germany. The cyclicality of the employment-to-population ratio is somewhat greater for
women than for men, but the differences are not statistically significant.

In the United States the cyclicality of the employment-to-population
ratio is slightly greater for men than for women. There, while the
cyclical movements of the labor force participation rate are greater for
women than for men, cyclical movements of the employment rate are
greater for men than for women. The effect of the latter outweighs the
effect of the former, and, on balance, male employment is more cyclical
than female employment.

As already noted, our findings on the variability of male and female
employment are likely to be sensitive to differences in the sectoral
distribution of male and female employment. Data on male and female
employment in industries for which output data are also available would
allow us to more directly assess the effects of employment adjustment
policies on the variability of male and female employment.

Some useful industry data for Germany are available on the gender
composition of employment. The data come from an establishment
survey conducted four times a year.[18] Although the industry definitions

18. Data sources are provided in appendix C.

Table 5-7. *Male versus Female Employment Elasticities, Germany, 1974–84*

Industry	Current quarter	One quarter	Two quarters	Four quarters	Six quarters
Nonelectrical machinery					
Male	0.021*	0.070*	0.138*	0.280*	0.386*
Female	0.078	0.179	0.293	0.515	0.617
Autos					
Male	0.042	0.092	0.143	0.290	0.339
Female	0.032	0.085	0.115	0.233	0.448
Stone, clay, and glass					
Male	0.039	0.088	0.157	0.316	0.437
Female	0.015	0.025	0.037	0.203	0.287
Electrical equipment					
Male	0.078	0.224	0.393	0.618*	0.699
Female	0.159	0.396	0.649	1.105	1.157
Paper					
Male	0.058	0.130	0.265	0.448	0.534
Female	0.071	0.214	0.328	0.592	0.786
Textiles					
Male	0.034	0.192	0.309	0.473	0.531
Female	0.039	0.095	0.214	0.473	0.598
Instruments					
Male	−0.028	0.033	0.269	0.660	1.050
Female	0.190	0.401	0.524	0.960	0.961
Apparel					
Male	−0.136	0.037	0.177	0.545	1.027
Female	0.080	0.206	0.439	0.758	0.826
Printing					
Male	0.074	0.129	0.172	0.322	0.554*
Female	0.112	0.311	0.449	0.641	1.293

*Male/female difference significant at 0.05 level.

in this survey differ somewhat from those used in the German monthly employer survey used in other analyses, we were able to match the data from the two surveys for a number of manufacturing industries. Using data on the percentages of nonproduction and production workers that are female from the quarterly survey and the total number of nonproduction and production workers from the monthly survey, we constructed a quarterly series of male and female employment by industry. The U.S. establishment survey that we use above to estimate production and nonproduction worker elasticities for manufacturing industries provides breakdowns of male and female employment. Unfortunately, it does not provide breakdowns by both sex and occupation.

Table 5-7 and table 5-8 present estimates of male and female employment adjustment by industry for Germany and the United States,

Table 5-8. Male versus Female Employment Elasticities, United States, 1974–84

Industry	Current quarter	One quarter	Two quarters	Four quarters	Six quarters
Nonelectrical machinery					
Male	0.482	0.654*	0.816*	0.846*	0.905*
Female	0.335	0.478	0.601	0.674	0.656
Primary metals					
Male	0.331	0.572	0.581	0.663	0.728
Female	0.395	0.648	0.657	0.748	0.891*
Autos					
Male	0.340	0.461	0.535	0.594	0.568
Female	0.378	0.597*	0.697*	0.850*	0.800*
Stone, clay, and glass					
Male	0.258	0.505	0.551	0.687	0.628
Female	0.239	0.536	0.611	0.756	0.646
Electrical equipment					
Male	0.253	0.484	0.557	0.550	0.508
Female	0.381*	0.710*	0.786*	0.794*	0.605
Paper					
Male	0.155	0.284	0.305	0.294	0.378
Female	0.248	0.476*	0.539*	0.497*	0.669*
Textiles					
Male	0.172	0.329	0.403	0.253	0.337
Female	0.227	0.444*	0.458	0.348	0.417
Instruments					
Male	0.124	0.235	0.348	0.499	0.526
Female	0.181	0.337*	0.379	0.471	0.500
Leather					
Male	0.160	0.299	0.266	0.209	0.118
Female	0.189	0.376	0.334	0.325	0.247
Apparel					
Male	0.065	0.135	0.296	0.314	0.329
Female	0.107	0.277	0.451	0.413	0.374
Printing					
Male	0.014	0.045	0.060	0.142	0.195
Female	0.034	0.093	0.157	0.108	0.261

*Male/female difference significant at 0.05 level.

respectively. The estimates reported in these tables suggest that, in a number of industries in both countries, the adjustment of female employment is greater than that of male employment, particularly over shorter time horizons, though the differences in many cases are not large. Unfortunately, probably because the German employment numbers are constructed using data from two sources, the standard errors of the German point estimates are quite large. In three out of the nine industries for which we were able to construct estimates of employment adjustment by sex, however, there is some evidence of significantly greater female adjustment. We also estimated employment elasticities for German male and female production workers. These estimates produced qualitatively similar results. For the United States, tests show that in six out of eleven industries, female employment adjustment is significantly greater than male employment adjustment, at least over some time horizons.

Because of the imprecision of the German estimates, we have used these quarterly industry data to calculate the simple correlation between the percent of employment that is female and the logarithm of shipments, using seasonally adjusted and detrended data. This correlation was large, positive, and significant for a majority of industries in both countries, indicating that female employment is more cyclically sensitive than male employment. Together with the employment elasticity estimates in tables 5-7 and 5-8, these results suggest that in both countries female employment is more responsive to changes in shipments in a number of industries, though, as noted, we have only rather imprecise estimates of employment adjustment by sex for Germany. There is, however, again no evidence to support the claim that German women are more vulnerable to layoff than are women in the United States. [19]

Foreign Workers

Foreign workers are likely to bear a disproportionate amount of the adjustment to changes in demand conditions. The reasons are varied. In Germany, the government explicitly has used immigration policy to increase the supply of workers when labor markets are tight and to reduce labor supply when unemployment is high. In addition, foreign workers are likely to hold lower-skilled positions and so to be at greater risk of being laid off during a downturn. They may be the target of

19. Had we looked at data for an earlier period, the evidence of greater female employment adjustment might have been stronger for both countries. Evidence reported by Deutschmann (1982) using annual data for 1960 through 1978 suggests that, even controlling for skill level, female employment in many German manufacturing industries was more responsive to changes in shipments than male employment in the same industry. Our own earlier work (Houseman and Abraham [1990]) indicates that, in many U.S. manufacturing industries, the responsiveness of female employment to changes in shipments was greater than that of male employment during the 1970s but has been about the same in recent years.

prejudice that makes them more susceptible to job loss and makes it more difficult for them to find a job during a recession.

The German economy has always been highly dependent on foreign labor. Following World War II, West Germany experienced rapid economic growth, and domestic labor was in short supply. An elastic supply of foreign labor helped moderate German wages. From the end of World War II until the erection of the Berlin Wall in 1961, the foreign workers in West Germany were predominantly refugees from Eastern Europe. These workers were highly skilled and easily assimilated into the population. Subsequently, so-called guest workers, who were primarily from Turkey, Yugoslavia, Italy, Greece, and Spain, replaced refugees as the main source of foreign labor. These guest workers tended to be less educated than previous waves of foreign entrants, and they primarily filled unskilled positions in the manufacturing sector of the economy.[20]

German policy toward guest workers has always been explicitly and solely an economic tool to control the labor supply. In fact, Germany does not formally allow any immigration, except of ethnic Germans from Eastern Europe. By treaty, citizens of other member states in the European Community are allowed free movement in Germany. Otherwise, however, admission to the country has been strictly controlled for the purpose of meeting labor shortages.

While the influx of guest workers helped ease labor shortages in Germany in the 1960s and early 1970s, guest workers served as a buffer for domestic workers during the recessions of the mid-1970s and 1980s. Table 5-9 compares the unemployment rates of foreign workers with those of all workers in Germany from 1970 to 1990.[21] Until the 1974–75 recession, the unemployment rate of foreign workers was somewhat lower than that of domestic workers. From 1973 to 1975 the unemployment rate of foreign workers jumped 6 percentage points from 0.8 percent to 6.8 percent; over the same period the unemployment rate for all workers in Germany rose 3.5 percentage points, from 1.2 percent to 4.7 percent. During the second half of the 1970s and throughout the

20. According to recent figures, about 80 percent of foreign workers in Germany work in manufacturing, primarily in the least-skilled, lowest-paid positions (Weiss 1987, p. 109).

21. These unemployment rates are official German statistics based on the number of persons registered with the employment service. While the reported rates are higher than unemployment rates using U.S. definitions would be, there is no reason to believe that the relative unemployment rates of foreign workers are distorted.

Table 5-9. *Trends in Unemployment of Foreign Workers, Germany,*
1970–90
Percent of labor force

Year	Total	Foreign workers
1970	0.7	0.3
1971	0.8	0.6
1972	1.1	0.7
1973	1.2	0.8
1974	2.6	2.9
1975	4.7	6.8
1976	4.6	5.1
1977	4.5	4.9
1978	4.3	5.3
1979	3.8	4.7
1980	3.8	5.0
1981	5.5	8.2
1982	7.5	11.9
1983	9.1	14.7
1984	9.1	14.0
1985	9.3	13.9
1986	9.0	13.7
1987	8.9	14.3
1988	8.7	14.4
1989	7.9	12.2
1990	7.2	10.9

Source: The reported unemployment rates are official German statistics based on employment service registrations and published by the Bundesanstalt für Arbeit.

1980s, foreign workers continued to experience much higher than average unemployment. From 1983 through 1988, unemployment of foreign workers hovered around 14 percent, about 5 percentage points above the overall unemployment rate. The foreign worker unemployment rate was still almost 4 percentage points above the overall rate in 1990.

The unemployment rate understates the impact of slack markets on foreign workers, for many foreigners who are unemployed or underemployed return to their home country. All new recruitment of guest workers has been banned since 1973. In 1983 the German government sought to more actively encourage outmigration of foreigners who were unemployed or who had been on short time for at least six months by providing them with substantial severance payments if they agreed to leave the country with their families.

The results of this policy, coupled with growing unemployment in the 1970s and 1980s, are clear in net migration statistics (figure 5-3).

Figure 5-3. *Net Migration of Foreigners, Germany, 1960–88*

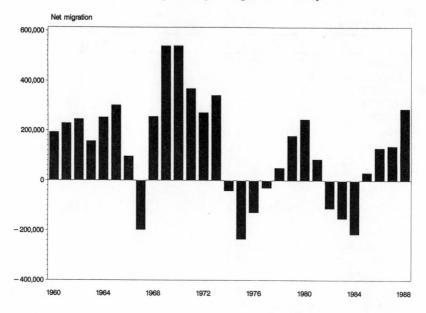

During the 1960s and early 1970s, Germany experienced huge inflows of foreign workers in most years, reflecting generally rapid growth and a healthy economy. The exceptions occurred during the 1967–68 recession years. During the recession in the mid-1970s there were again sizable outflows of foreign workers. Net migration became moderately positive during the recovery in the late 1970s, but turned negative again in the early 1980s.[22] The outmigration of foreign workers from Germany and the high unemployment rate of foreign workers who stayed are reflected in the declining share of employment in Germany accounted for by foreign workers during this period (figure 5-4). Net foreign migration rebounded in the late 1980s, and the foreign share of employment had risen slightly by the end of the decade.

Immigration policy has been much less tied to economic policy and

22. Even though there was no new recruitment of foreign labor after 1973, family members were allowed to join workers already in the country. Entry of family members accounts for the positive net migration observed during the late 1970s. Until very recently, spouses of foreign workers had to reside in Germany for four years before being given free access to the labor market, though they were allowed to take a job sooner if no European Community national was available to fill the position. Special rules also govern the right of foreign workers' children to work in Germany, though children of foreigners who have grown up in Germany have essentially the same employment rights as German nationals.

Figure 5-4. *Percent of Employment Accounted for by Foreign Workers, Germany, 1974–90*

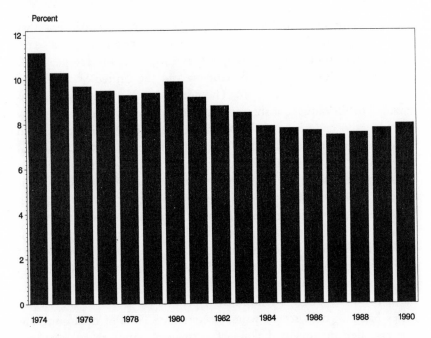

labor market conditions in the United States. Legal immigration into the United States is subject to annual quotas. Workers with skills in short supply have been given varying preference in recent history. The Immigration and Nationality Act of 1952 gave highly skilled immigrants top priority. But the Immigration Acts of 1965 and 1976 deemphasized labor skills and instead gave preference to those with family ties in the United States. Immigration legislation passed in 1990 again increases the emphasis on labor market considerations. Visas will be set aside for individuals with "exceptional ability" or with professional degrees and other skills. The legislation also sets aside visas for investors who would create at least ten jobs. This new emphasis on labor market considerations is a response to a perceived shortage of highly educated and skilled individuals and to the belief that the United States must compete with other countries for this type of individual to be successful in a global economy.

Quotas on the number of permanent immigrants are set in legislation and are adjusted infrequently. Many more people would like to enter the United States as permanent immigrants than are allowed to do so legally. Although documented immigration flows do change with economic conditions, they are not particularly sensitive to the state of the economy.[23]

Under some circumstances, nonimmigrants are awarded visas that allow them to work temporarily in the United States. A special temporary worker program, popularly referred to as the bracero program, under which Mexicans could be employed in the United States was in force between 1942 and 1964. The admission of these workers was intended to alleviate labor shortages in selected occupations, particularly agricultural occupations. At its peak, as many as half a million Mexican workers a year entered the U.S. labor market under this controversial program. It is suspected that many of these people remained in the United States as illegal immigrants after the program was discontinued.[24] Current law allows the issuance of temporary work visas to foreign nationals in several categories. The most important of these groups are individuals of distinguished merit and ability; persons who fill temporary positions, such as seasonal agricultural jobs, for which employers have unsuccessfully tried to recruit domestic applicants; exchange visitors who come to study, teach, observe, and so on; and intra-company transferees. Although the number of persons admitted in these categories has grown in recent years, documented flows of nonimmigrant workers, like documented flows of permanent immigrants, have not been especially cyclical.[25]

The flow of illegal immigrants is probably sensitive to economic conditions in the United States, though, by its nature, illegal immigration is impossible to document with any precision. Barry Chiswick estimates that in 1986 there were "as many as 4 million illegal alien workers, comprising 4 percent of the U.S. labor force."[26] These workers come primarily from Mexico and other Latin American countries. A large percentage, it is believed, move in and out of the United States each year. Although the Immigration Reform and Control Act of 1986 was intended to drastically reduce illegal immigration by introducing sanctions against employers that hire illegal aliens and by increasing enforcement, it is widely believed that large numbers continue to im-

23. Boyd (1976, p. 86) shows that even in comparison to Canada, a country that has similar immigration policies, U.S. immigration has been unresponsive to economic conditions.

24. Briggs (1986, pp. 998–99).

25. See U.S. Department of Labor (1989, pp. 42–3).

26. Chiswick (1988, p. 2).

migrate to the United States illegally each year. The extent to which this illegal supply of labor buffers or displaces U.S. workers during recessions is unknown.

Conclusion

We began our discussion of distributional issues by characterizing labor adjustment practices in Germany as more equitable than those in the United States. Compared with American companies, German companies, in general, rely more on adjusting average hours per worker rather than hiring and firing workers to adjust labor input to demand changes. This greater reliance on average hours adjustment helps to dampen fluctuations in employment and spread adjustment costs across a larger number of workers.

Although greater reliance on adjustment of average hours per worker helps to stabilize employment against demand shocks and spread the adjustment across workers, these practices cannot protect all workers against all shocks. German companies regularly lay off workers and in the aggregate Germany has experienced large fluctuations in employment and high unemployment in recent years. Some observers have claimed that the German institutional structure imposes a disproportionate share of the burden of adjustment on youth, women, and foreigners. In examining the cyclicality of employment, unemployment, and labor force participation by demographic group, however, we found the effects of labor adjustment more evenly spread across age groups in Germany compared with the United States and no strong evidence that German women bear a proportionately greater amount of adjustment to demand fluctuations than do American women.

Although younger workers in Germany, like younger workers in the United States, appear to bear a disproportionate amount of adjustment to fluctuations in demand, differences in the volatility of employment, unemployment, and labor force participation across age groups in Germany are generally smaller than in the United States and often statistically insignificant. In recent years employment reductions in Germany have been shifted to some extent onto older workers through government-subsidized early retirement schemes. Whether it is desirable to shift adjustment onto older workers in this fashion is debatable. Early retirement programs generally have been viewed as a mechanism for painlessly reducing the work force. Insofar as older workers can be induced to retire voluntarily, layoffs of younger workers may be avoided and the job prospects of labor market entrants may be enhanced. The maintenance of career continuity for younger workers may have positive long-run effects on the development of their skills. There have, however, been allegations that some older workers have been coerced to participate in early retirement schemes that made them substantially worse off. In addition, the potential economic contributions of older workers are lost permanently when they retire.

We also find no strong support for the hypothesis that women bear a larger share of adjustment in Germany than in the United States. In the aggregate the cyclicality of female employment is somewhat greater than that of male employment in Germany; in the aggregate it is somewhat less in the United States. When we look at employment adjustment patterns in particular industries, we do find that for a number of industries in both countries the adjustment of female employment is greater than that of male employment, but the differences in many industries are not large. Overall, German policies do not seem to result in a less equitable distribution of the burden of adjustment by sex than occurs in the unregulated U.S. economy.

The sharp rise in the unemployment rates of women and workers in their late fifties coupled with the sharp decline in the labor force participation rates of teenagers and persons in their sixties during the 1970s and 1980s might have led one to suspect that youth, older workers, and women absorb a disproportionate amount of adjustment to fluctuations in demand conditions in Germany. However, the rise in unemployment and decline in labor force participation among these groups appears instead to represent a secular trend, most likely reflecting at least in part the slow trend growth in employment experienced by the German economy throughout the period. As noted in chapter 3, many reasons have been offered for the stagnation of employment in Germany during the 1970s and 1980s, but we argue that regulation of layoffs was not an important contributing factor.

We do find somewhat stronger evidence that foreign workers, who filled primarily low-skill jobs when tight labor markets prevailed in the 1960s and early 1970s in Germany, have helped buffer domestic workers from the adverse economic conditions that prevailed in the mid-1970s and 1980s. However, the importance of guest workers in the German economy has diminished and will continue to diminish as workers from the old East Germany and immigrants from other Eastern European countries displace foreign workers from the Mediterranean basin. Unlike guest workers, this new group of Eastern European labor will not serve the same buffer function to workers in the old West Germany.

In the United States the extensive use of layoffs rather than hours reductions shifts the burden of adjustment onto certain groups of workers. Youth, in particular, bear the brunt of adjustment to downturns in the United States. Although white-collar workers are frequently laid off, and some evidence suggests that they have become more vulnerable to layoff in recent years, white-collar workers have received much stronger job security than have blue-collar workers in the United States. This fact raises questions about why adjustment differs so much across occupations in the United States and whether blue-collar workers can be given greater job protection.

The difference in adjustment between blue- and white-collar workers is often explained on technological grounds. The firm's demand for production workers is much more tied to the level of production than is its demand for nonproduction workers. Certainly technological factors explain some of the difference.

Another explanation focuses on institutional aspects of the organization of work. According to this view, whereas blue-collar workers usually have rigid task assignments, white-collar workers are expected to be flexible in the tasks they perform. In return for this flexibility, they receive an implied promise of job security. Although differences in personnel policies for blue- and white-collar workers could be ascribed to technological factors, some have argued that the personnel practices for white-collar workers can and should be applied to blue-collar workers, as well. Germany is held as an example of a country in which this has been successfully done.[27]

27. See Osterman (1988). Sengenberger (1985) contains a useful discussion of the trade-off between internal and external flexibility in various OECD countries.

CHAPTER SIX

Lessons for U.S. Policy

THE UNITED STATES stands out among industrialized countries in the extent to which its companies hire and fire workers in response to fluctuations in demand. As a consequence of these practices, jobs in America tend to be far less secure than in other countries, and the burden of adjustment to demand fluctuations falls on workers who are laid off. Through an in-depth comparison of adjustment practices in Germany and the United States, we have sought to explore the advantages—and disadvantages—of another approach in which companies rely more on hours reduction, attrition, and other alternatives to layoff.

Should U.S. policy be reformed to encourage greater use of alternatives to layoff and thereby promote job security for American workers? We believe the answer is a qualified yes. Current U.S. policy contains a clear pro-layoff bias. Perhaps most important, the existence of an imperfectly experience-rated unemployment insurance system that permits payment of benefits to workers on layoff but not, in general, to workers whose hours have been reduced encourages reliance on layoffs rather than work sharing. In addition, laid-off workers may lose their health insurance coverage, becoming a drain on the medicaid system and the private health care system as nonpaying patients. The fact that the health care costs of laid-off workers are at least partially absorbed by third parties may encourage excessive reliance on layoffs. Excessive use of layoffs results in an unnecessary loss of firm-specific worker skills and a corresponding reduction in productivity in the economy. Less reliance on layoffs and more reliance on work sharing would help to spread the costs and risks of adjustment across groups of workers and is thus desirable on equity grounds.

Opponents of stronger job security policies, however, have raised legitimate concerns about their effects on American business. Such policies, it is feared, will hamper necessary adjustment, will be costly for companies, and ultimately will raise unemployment and inhibit growth. Our analysis of the German and U.S. manufacturing sectors indicates that even stringent restrictions on layoffs have not had serious adverse effects on German business. Although German companies use fewer layoffs to reduce labor input during downturns, in most cases they compensate in the short run through greater reductions in average hours per worker. Through attrition, early retirement, and job buyouts, as well as layoffs, the adjustment of employment levels to a decline in demand typically catches up with that in the corresponding American industry in four to six quarters. Although Germany did experience high unemployment levels during the 1980s, our findings complement those of other research that has concluded that regulation of layoffs did not contribute significantly to Germany's unemployment problem.[1]

The finding that German policies promoting alternatives to layoff are not harmful for the German economy, of course, does not imply that we should adopt German policies in this country. Because of differences in the two countries' industrial relations systems, policies that work well in Germany may not work well in the United States. While we advocate the introduction of policies in the United States designed to correct existing biases that favor layoffs and to promote the use of alternatives to layoffs, we do not advocate the wholesale adoption of German labor market policies or indeed of any other country's policies. Rather, we advocate the adoption of selected policies compatible with existing U.S. industrial relations.

Trends in U.S. Policy

In response to the question of whether U.S. labor policy should be moving in the direction of German policy, one could argue that it already is. The 1980s were a period of heightened public concern about job security issues and some significant policy measures intended to increase worker job security were introduced during those years. By the end of the decade, fourteen states had adopted legislation allowing workers on short time to collect prorated unemployment insurance benefits; most of these laws were passed during the early 1980s. In 1988

1. See, in particular, Flanagan (1987).

Congress passed the first federal legislation requiring employers to provide workers with advance notice before a mass layoff. These policy initiatives address key areas in which U.S. and German labor market policy traditionally have differed: the availability of benefits for workers on short time and restrictions on layoff. They arguably have moved U.S. policy somewhat closer to the German model.

Short-time Compensation

Although layoffs are the dominant form of adjustment for blue-collar workers in the United States today, this has not always been true. Before World War II, work-sharing schemes were a much more common response to excess labor during recessions.[2] Interestingly, work-sharing schemes were especially prevalent in unionized firms.[3] Available statistics suggest that work sharing grew substantially during the Great Depression. Work sharing was promoted by both the Hoover and Roosevelt administrations and by private business groups, which reasoned that if private business could mitigate unemployment on its own, it could avert the enactment of liberal legislation such as that establishing unemployment insurance.

Organized labor also supported work sharing. As the depression wore on, however, labor's view of work sharing soured. Few firms offered any assistance to workers on short time. Workers on short time suffered large pay cuts that often reduced their earnings below subsistence levels. Consequently, work sharing during the Great Depression became widely viewed as a failed experiment.[4]

Following the depression, there was a gradual shift away from work sharing toward layoffs as the preferred method of adjustment in union establishments. Near the end of the depression unions began to move away from supporting unlimited work sharing in favor of a two-step process whereby hours were initially reduced to some minimum level, after which layoffs occurred. Sanford M. Jacoby writes that unionized establishments gradually shifted away from this two-step procedure in favor of just layoffs over the next twenty years.[5] A major factor causing this shift was the introduction of unemployment insurance. As unem-

2. See, for example, Carter and Sutch (1991).
3. According to Jacoby (1985, p. 28) the early unions favored work sharing over layoffs because demand in many industries was so volatile that a layoff policy based on seniority would have pitted union members with jobs against those without jobs.
4. Nemirow (1984, p. 163).
5. See Jacoby (1985, p. 247).

ployment benefits were liberalized and as unions were able to negotiate supplemental unemployment benefits from employers, layoffs became more acceptable.[6]

Thus, the introduction of unemployment insurance in the United States introduced a serious, possibly unintentional, bias toward the use of layoffs in lieu of work sharing. The same did not occur in Germany, for benefits for short-time work have always been a part of the unemployment insurance system there.

In recent years, a number of states have sought to encourage greater use of work sharing by making prorated unemployment insurance benefits available to workers whose hours have been cut, under certain circumstances. Initial reviews of these programs, however, have been mixed. The most comprehensive study to date of short-time compensation (STC) programs in the United States was done by Mathematica Policy Research (MPR) for the U.S. Department of Labor.[7] That study found that participating employers and employees generally were satisfied with the program. The study's most critical conclusion was that participation in STC programs did not reduce the incidence of layoffs, though the validity of that finding was questioned by the study's advisory panel.

Perhaps most disturbing is the simple fact that U.S. employers have used available STC programs very little. This fact raises the question of why use in the United States has been so low relative to the use of similar programs in Germany and other countries. Is there something fundamental about American institutions that makes such a program less viable here than abroad? Or are there problems in the way that states have implemented these programs that have discouraged their use? We believe the answer is, at least in part, the latter.

One frequently mentioned deterrent to the use of short-time work is the cost to employers of maintaining fringe benefits. Although state laws generally do not require U.S. employers to maintain fringe benefits in order to participate in short-time compensation programs, most choose to do so.[8] In contrast, employers who lay off workers typically discontinue their benefits coverage.

6. The same shift toward layoffs did not occur in the nonunion sector during this period. Medoff (1979) has shown that even in recent years layoffs have been more common in union establishments.

7. Kerachsky and others (1985).

8. Only five states—Arkansas, Louisiana, Massachusetts, New York, and Washington—require employers to maintain some or all fringe benefits for workers in STC programs. See Vroman (1990). This requirement is similar to the requirement imposed

Although fringe benefit costs are likely to be higher for employers using short time in lieu of layoffs, other labor costs are likely to be lower. Employers who use short time will save on hiring and training costs if the downturn is temporary, since fewer of their workers will take other jobs and have to be replaced when the upturn begins. In addition, because both lower-paid junior workers and higher-paid senior workers may have their hours reduced under work sharing, whereas layoffs are concentrated among lower-paid junior workers, work sharing may produce greater wage savings than a layoff. Whether this occurs, however, will depend on the productivity of junior and senior workers relative to their wages. The labor cost savings associated with short-time work compared with layoffs also depend on how the implementation of short-time work affects productivity. Some have argued that short-time work improves employee morale, while it avoids the costly "bumping" procedures associated with a seniority-based layoff. These productivity effects are likely to vary across establishments, however, and are largely unstudied.[9]

The structure of unemployment insurance taxes in many states offering STC is another potential deterrent to the use of work sharing instead of layoffs. Many states that have implemented an STC program initially were concerned about the effects it would have on the unemployment insurance trust fund. As noted earlier, as of the start of 1991 seven of the fourteen states with STC programs still had special financing provisions for STC or placed limitations on the use of STC. Five states assess higher tax rates on certain companies that use short time, always including those at the regular maximum unemployment insurance tax rate. In two states employers with negative account balances cannot use STC programs at all.

---

on German employers that social insurance contributions be maintained at their usual level during a period of short-time work. In fact, because German employers must cover the worker's share of health insurance contributions on the difference between normal and short-time earnings, German employers' hourly nonwage costs may increase during a period of short-time work.

9. In a survey reported in Kerachsky and others (1985, pp. 74, 77, 79), employers who participated in an STC program were asked what they felt were its advantages and disadvantages. A number of employers listed as advantages effects that might be expected to enhance worker productivity in the short or long run: maintaining valued employees (50.0 percent); maintaining employee morale (14.8 percent); avoiding disruptions to business operations (11.2 percent); and flexibility to adjust employment to levels of demand (8.9 percent). Among the disadvantages, only 8.2 percent listed inefficiency in the production process. In a comparison group of employers who did not use STC programs, the percent citing inefficiency in the production process was not much different (10.2 percent).

This bias against the use of work sharing arguably is greatest for employers who, from society's perspective, should be most encouraged to use short time. Employers who have relied extensively on layoffs in the past to adjust the work force and who are at the maximum unemployment insurance tax rate face no additional tax cost if they continue to use layoffs; however, they may substantially increase their tax costs if they switch to work-sharing schemes, if they are allowed to participate in the programs at all. Yet, employers with a history of using layoffs, especially temporary layoffs, are exactly the employers that this policy is trying to target.

The use of STC programs also may be low because employers lack information on these programs, because they are reluctant to change established personnel practices, or because they view state requirements associated with the use of STC programs as a burden. Some have argued that use of STC programs in states with such programs has been low largely because many employers are ignorant of them. The MPR study used a comparison group methodology to analyze the effects of STC programs in California, Arizona, and Oregon. Outcomes for firms that used the STC programs were compared with those for a matched group of employers that did not. Interestingly, only half of the employers in that study's comparison group knew of the STC program. The employers in the comparison group were selected to have characteristics similar to those of employers who used STC and, in theory, should have had a similar need for the program.

Even if they are aware of STC programs, managers may be uncertain of the effects of using work-sharing schemes on their costs, and consequently hesitant to experiment with them. As we have discussed, companies in the United States traditionally have tried to offer their white-collar workers employment security. With STC programs, employers could continue to provide employment security for white-collar workers while cutting labor costs, at least in the short run. However, we might expect employers to be more reluctant to introduce STC programs for their blue-collar employees, for this would mean a fundamental change in personnel policies. One puzzling finding of the MPR study was that firms participating in STC programs used layoffs to the same extent as comparison-group firms; thus, firms using STC cut total hours more. Wayne Vroman has speculated that the answer to this puzzle may be that firms using STC offered it primarily for their white-collar workers. [10]

Red tape associated with implementing an STC program also may

10. Vroman (1990).

inhibit its use. Under current state laws, the administrative procedures required to initiate an STC program are more burdensome than those required to implement a layoff. To initiate short time, a company must get approval from its union, if it has one, and from the state. States may require such information as exactly which workers will be placed on short time, the percentage by which these workers' hours will be reduced, and the expected duration of short-time work. Companies are likely to be uncertain of their need for work sharing, even over relatively short periods. In Germany, companies have considerable discretion to change the assignment of employees to short time and the hours these employees work once a basic plan is approved. In the United States, any modifications to the STC plan generally must be approved, and state governments may be unwilling to approve a flexible plan that allows week-to-week changes in which workers are placed on short time and what hours they work.[11] Such approval and reporting requirements may be—or at least may be perceived as—burdensome to companies and deter them from considering the short-time option. In contrast, if a layoff is temporary or affects less than a third of its work force, the company does not even have to provide advance notice of its plans.

Several of the obstacles to the use of short time just mentioned—lack of information on the STC option, uncertainty about how the use of short time would work out, and administrative hurdles associated with the use of short-time compensation—are likely to become less serious as experience with the programs grows. First and perhaps most important, the dissemination of information about a new program simply takes time. Companies that are fearful of trying something new may be encouraged by other companies' successful experiences with work sharing. Our interviews with employment service personnel in states that have short-time programs suggest that experience with the programs has led to improvements in program administration. In one state, for example, employers used to be required to list all of the workers who would be receiving short-time compensation before their short-time plan could be approved; this requirement was subsequently deemed unnecessary and has been dropped.

Thus far, we have focused on reasons why employers might oppose the implementation of short time to avoid layoffs. But in certain cases,

---

11. For example, we are aware of one company whose short-time plan was turned down by a state because the company wanted to rotate workers in and out of short time, and the state believed the plan was too complex for the state to administer it.

workers may oppose work-sharing schemes too. Seniority-based layoff rules, which are especially prevalent in unionized establishments, protect senior workers from job or income loss. Although the availability of short-time compensation makes work sharing more acceptable to senior workers, they still may suffer substantial reductions in pay unless their employer supplements state benefits.

There may be little social pressure on workers to accept work-sharing schemes if it is not in their own interest, for the use of seniority-based layoffs has become widely accepted as a fair way of allocating adjustment costs in the United States. In writing on the historical evolution of seniority-based layoffs, Jacoby claims that "the shift to straight layoffs can also be explained by the unionized sector's growing acceptance of seniority as an equitable principle of distribution. After [World War II], unionized workers were more likely than nonunion workers to be affected by seniority in a variety of ways, from promotions to parking privileges. They became accustomed to regarding seniority as fair, even though it slighted need and merit."[12] Organized labor generally has supported legislation enacting short-time compensation. However, it might be expected that senior workers would oppose the implementation of work-sharing schemes in some cases.

Though clearly some important questions must be answered about the low usage of short-time compensation in states with STC programs, interestingly the use of short time has risen during the most recent recession. Unpublished figures compiled by the Unemployment Insurance Service of the Department of Labor indicate that, nationally, the share of initial unemployment insurance claims accounted for by work sharing roughly doubled between January 1989 and January 1991; the same is true of weeks of benefits paid. As discussed in the following pages, we believe that introduction of appropriately structured short-time programs in states that do not currently have them, together with policies that make layoffs less attractive, could lead to a significant increase in work sharing by U.S. employers.

Advance Notice

The first U.S. law requiring advance notice before a mass layoff or plant closure took effect in 1989. Evidence from several recent studies indicates that advance notice of layoff significantly reduces the expected

12. Jacoby (1985, p. 247).

duration of post-displacement joblessness.[13] Paul Swaim and Michael Podgursky, for example, estimate that providing 60 days' advance notice to displaced workers reduces their expected joblessness by two to four weeks, with larger effects for workers who lose their jobs because of a plant closing.[14] And Christopher J. Ruhm finds that the advantages of prior notification are particularly great for household heads, married persons, and workers living in areas of high unemployment. These are all groups for whom spells of joblessness are likely to have particularly serious consequences.[15]

Thus far, evidence suggests that the cost to U.S. business of the advance notice requirement is minimal. The chief fear that many U.S. businesses had about the legislation's effects was that it would spur much costly litigation by workers who had been laid off and who believed they had not received proper notice. Although the experience with this law is too limited to judge its effects fully, in the first year of its implementation relatively little litigation was reported.[16]

U.S. law requiring that employers provide workers with sixty days of notice before a mass layoff is weak compared with regulations governing layoffs in Germany. Unlike German law, U.S. law does not require consultation with worker representatives or any form of compensation to workers who are laid off. The thresholds defining a mass layoff are much higher in the United States than in Germany, and the U.S. advance notice requirements do not apply to temporary layoffs.

The German experience has shown that even far more stringent regulations can be enacted without harming industry in any obvious way. But the effects of more stringent regulations might be different in the United States than they are in Germany. We have emphasized that Germany has important supporting policies and industrial relations institutions that help make such regulations viable. For example, compensation for short-time work and subsidies for early retirement help to reduce the costs to companies of using alternatives to layoff. Social plan

13. See Addison and Portugal (1987); Podgursky and Swaim (1987); Ehrenberg and Jakubson (1988); Ruhm (1989); and Swaim and Podgursky (1990).

14. Most of the beneficial effect of advance notice on jobless duration estimated by Swaim and Podgursky (1990, esp. p. 167) reflects the reduction in the probability that a displaced worker enters joblessness. The distinction between the effect of advance notice on the probability that a displaced worker experiences any joblessness and the effect of advance notice on the length of spells of joblessness once they have begun is also emphasized by Ehrenberg and Jakubson (1988) and Ruhm (1989).

15. Ruhm (1989).

16. See Samborn (1990).

requirements are workable only because of the existence of works councils, with representatives who are knowledgeable about company finances and can effectively negotiate with management over compensation for laid-off workers.

In sum, policies cannot always be transferred easily from one country to another. In certain cases policies should not be adopted individually, but rather as a part of a set of interrelated measures. In other cases policies from another country may not be suited for the United States at all because of differences in the two countries' industrial relations. Given this caveat, the German experience provides some important lessons—positive and negative—for U.S. policy.

New Directions for U.S. Policy

Our recommendations follow from the observation that the current structure of U.S. policy leads to greater reliance on layoffs than is socially desirable. In part, this situation reflects the structure of the U.S. unemployment insurance system. In making their layoff decisions, U.S. employers also do not consider the burden that laid-off workers will impose on the health care system and third-parties' pocketbooks. Moreover, concern for equity dictates encouraging greater reliance on work sharing rather than layoffs.

We recommend three sets of policies to correct the excessive reliance on layoffs. The first set of policies includes positive incentives to encourage greater use of work sharing rather than layoffs, when appropriate. The second set provides disincentives for employers to make excessive use of layoffs in reducing labor during downturns. Finally, based on the German experience, we point to the important, though indirect, benefits that policies encouraging greater training in the workplace can have on worker job security.

Incentives for Work Sharing

To help eliminate the encouragement of layoffs built into our unemployment insurance system, all states should be required to offer pro-rated benefits for workers on short time.[17] Moreover, apparent problems

17. All states do offer partial unemployment benefits to workers with very low earnings. As discussed earlier, however, these programs are not designed to support work-sharing schemes.

with existing STC programs should be tackled. We believe the low usage of these programs to date is largely attributable to the way these programs have been implemented, rather than to any basic flaw in the programs' conception.

To increase the use of work sharing, state governments should eliminate the less favorable tax treatment and special eligibility requirements imposed on employers who wish to use the STC program. Half of the states with STC programs have some form of tax penalty or limit coverage for the use of short-time work. Given the social benefits of work sharing over layoffs, these differences between the treatment of short time and layoffs should be eliminated. This objective could be achieved without undermining state unemployment insurance trust funds by tightening the experience rating of employers' tax contributions for unemployment insurance.

For many companies, the cost of maintaining fringe benefits may be another significant deterrent to using work-sharing schemes. Even when state laws do not require businesses participating in STC programs to maintain fringe benefits, it may be administratively difficult for companies to cut benefits temporarily. Moreover, the loss of health insurance by dislocated workers has been a major problem in this country, resulting in personal hardship and a drain on the medicaid and private health care systems.[18] U.S. policy should encourage businesses to maintain these benefits for workers on short time. If the United States moves more aggressively toward publicly provided health care, then the costs of providing health insurance for workers on short time may become less of a burden to businesses, depending on how a national health insurance scheme is financed.[19] In the meantime, states should offer companies subsidies or loans to help cover the costs of maintaining fringe benefits, especially health insurance coverage. Such assistance would help companies retain valued employees and help them over short-term liquidity problems. State subsidies of health insurance for workers on short time would be compensated, at least in part, by lower expenditures on medicaid.

18. For a discussion of the incidence of the loss of benefits by dislocated workers see Flaim and Sehgal (1985).

19. If the publicly provided health insurance is financed by a payroll tax with a low ceiling on taxable wages, then the costs of health insurance—or health insurance taxes—would continue to represent a fixed cost of employment in most cases. If, however, there were a high ceiling on taxable wages and no special requirements were introduced for payment of national health insurance contributions by employers using short time, then health taxes would be reduced in most cases when hours were cut.

In addition, state governments should make greater efforts to ensure that business and labor groups are informed about the existence of STC programs and their potential benefits. In states that offer short-time compensation, survey evidence shows that many businesses are unaware of the program. Businesses that are aware of the program still may be uncertain about how they would implement a work-sharing scheme and what the ultimate costs of work sharing compared with layoffs would be; consequently, businesses may be reluctant to change established practices. The dissemination of more and better information on STC programs is simple and relatively inexpensive, but important for the success of these programs.

Finally, states should endeavor to streamline the administrative procedures required to implement an STC plan. By definition, a work-sharing plan used in place of a layoff will affect more workers and hence mean more paperwork for the company. Thus, it is especially important for states to keep reporting requirements to a minimum. States should make approval of STC plans quick and routine. As in Germany, employers should be given considerable latitude to alter the plan without prior government approval.

Disincentives to Layoffs

Short-time compensation programs directly encourage greater use of work sharing. Another way to encourage the use of work sharing along with other alternatives to layoffs is to adopt policies that raise the cost of laying off workers. The United States has relied primarily on experience rating of employers' unemployment insurance taxes to inhibit excess layoffs. Although states vary in the degree of experience rating, the experience rating in all states is imperfect in the sense that the present value of the added unemployment insurance taxes that an employer pays as a consequence of laying off an additional worker is typically less than the present value of the unemployment benefits the worker receives.

The most important reason for imperfect experience rating under the current system is that many employers who make heavy use of layoffs are already paying the maximum possible unemployment insurance tax rate and thus incur no additional tax liability if they lay off another worker. In recent years, the maximum tax rate in most states' experience-rating schedules has risen significantly. Before 1985, the federal government required states to levy a maximum unemployment insurance tax rate of at least 2.7 percent on employers whose workers make heaviest use of the system; effective January 1, 1985, the required maximum unemployment insurance tax rate rose to 5.4 percent.[20] In 1978, the actual maximum unemployment insurance tax rate averaged 4.5 percent; by 1988, it had risen to 6.6 percent, an increase of 46 percent.

These increases in the maximum tax rate have been partially offset by reductions in the size of the taxable wage base relative to total wages paid, which have moved in tandem with average weekly benefits. The ratio of the taxable wage base to total wages is important because having a smaller taxable wage base reduces the maximum unemployment insurance tax liability associated with a given tax rate and thus increases the probability that a high-layoff employer will pay nothing toward the unemployment insurance outlay associated with laying off another worker. Between 1978 and 1988, the average ratio of taxable to total wages dropped from 50 percent to 39 percent, a 22 percent drop. Taking the increase in the maximum rate and the drop in the ratio of taxable to total wages into account, however, the net result has been a substantial increase in the degree of experience rating under the unemployment insurance system.

In states where a large share of unemployment benefits are still paid to workers laid off by employers already paying the maximum tax rate, further increases in the maximum tax rate are warranted. One way to ensure that the present degree of experience rating is not eroded would be to index the taxable wage base to average annual earnings in covered employment.

The advance notice requirements implemented in 1989 represent the first major regulation of layoffs in the United States. The U.S. notice requirements, however, are not stringent by international standards. Given that the benefits of advance notice to laid-off workers and their communities are potentially great, and that the regulation does not seem to have imposed a major burden on business, some extension of advance notice requirements is warranted. Under current law the thresholds defining a mass layoff are set too high. Large companies may still permanently lay off hundreds of workers without triggering notice requirements. The threshold defining a mass layoff should be lowered from one-third to 20 percent of the work force over a thirty-day period, and all permanent layoffs of 100 or more workers over a thirty-day period should be subject to advance notice requirements. Some mini-

20. Vroman (1989, pp. 3–5).

mum threshold, as exists in current law, could be retained to protect smaller companies. Even these suggested thresholds would still be much higher than those in Germany and most other countries.

Many countries, including Germany, also require companies to pay laid-off workers some form of compensation. Mandatory, negotiated severance payments, as required in Germany, are infeasible in the United States, which has no comprehensive system of worker representation. We recommend instead that U.S. employers be required to pay for continued health insurance coverage of workers they lay off for one to two months.[21] Clearly, some payment would have to be specified for employers who do not offer workers health insurance to avoid creating a disincentive for employers to offer health coverage, and the precise details of such a requirement would depend on the outcomes of proposed reforms to the U.S. health insurance system.

Incentives for Workplace Training

Our recommendations thus far have concerned policies that would directly affect employers' choices between layoffs and alternatives such as work sharing. In the German context, we pointed out that their extensive system of worker training contributes in indirect but important ways to job and income security in that country. For one thing, it is less costly for employers to offer job security to workers who have a broad set of skills. Rather than laying off excess workers, an employer can transfer them into positions vacated by those who retire or quit. Extensive use of internal transfers to avoid layoffs, however, is more feasible if the work force possesses a broad set of skills. Moreover, in the event of layoffs, highly trained workers are in a better position to find new employment.

According to one estimate, German employers spend roughly twice as much per worker annually on training as do U.S. employers. Company investments in apprenticeship training account for most of the difference in training expenditures between Germany and the United States.[22] German apprenticeship programs are developed jointly by industry, labor, and government representatives, and the costs of training are

21. Under current law, U.S. employers are required to give a laid-off employee the option of buying continued coverage under any group health plan in which he or she may have participated while employed, but are not required to pay for continued coverage.

22. Hilton (1991).

shared by employers' associations and state and federal government. The ability of employers to pool the costs and benefits of training through employers' associations, many believe, is critical to the high training investments in Germany. Such cooperation at the industry level is absent in the United States. This is widely believed to have led to inadequate private sector investment in worker training in this country, primarily because companies are likely to be reluctant to invest in workers who then may leave to work for competitors.

A recent report by the Office of Technology Assessment and a follow-up study by one of its authors, Margret Hilton, outline some policy options that would address this problem by encouraging U.S. firms to emulate the German approach to training.[23] One option would expand current funding from the U.S. Department of Labor to help establish industry consortia that would provide worker training. Another would clarify U.S. antitrust laws to facilitate greater cooperation among companies in an industry in the area of training. The adoption of such policies is desirable. More and better training of workers in the United States obviously would increase labor productivity. It would also enhance workers' employment security.

Conclusion

This set of recommendations concerning work sharing, layoffs, and workplace training, would build on existing U.S. policies. In some areas, particularly the regulation of layoffs, the recommended policies would be far weaker than those adopted by Germany and other countries. Combined, however, these policies should be effective in promoting alternatives to layoff and stronger job security for American workers without burdening business. In the case of Germany, we have emphasized the importance of linkages between labor market policies that, on the one hand, regulate layoffs and, on the other hand, subsidize alternatives. In the United States too, policies that would discourage layoffs through tax incentives or regulation should be accompanied by policies that ease the costs to companies of using alternatives through the introduction of STC programs and incentives for workplace training.

In trying to reduce worker dislocation, U.S. policy should seek to avoid some of the problems associated with certain aspects of German

23. U.S. Congress (1990); and Hilton (1991).

policy. For example, one of the dangers of protective legislation is that it will divide workers into two classes: those with protected, permanent jobs and those with little job security who absorb a grossly disproportionate amount of adjustment to economic shocks. German migration policy was explicitly designed to use foreign workers as a buffer.

There is also a risk that employers trying to circumvent protective legislation may create two classes of workers. In Germany, the relaxation of restrictions on the use of temporary workers has been associated with a large increase in this type of labor. In the United States, recent evidence suggesting that temporary employment is on the rise has generated concern over the quality and stability of jobs in this country. The implementation of policies to reduce layoffs, such as tighter experience rating of unemployment insurance taxes, could increase the use of temporary workers unless these policies are accompanied by measures to reduce the costs to employers of using short-time work or other alternatives.

In closing, we emphasize that public policies designed to promote alternatives to layoff or to mitigate the effects of dislocation are not a panacea for unemployment. Such policies can help to reduce unemployment and the high costs of dislocation to individuals and society at large. But worker dislocation, often on a large scale, is unavoidable and necessary for the economy to remain dynamic and competitive in world markets. Moreover, these policies address only one source of unemployment. Labor market policies are a complement, not a substitute, for macroeconomic policies designed to address problems of insufficient demand and trade and industrial policies designed to address inefficiencies elsewhere in the economy.

Technical Appendix to Chapter 4

T HE FOLLOWING PAGES contain a discussion of the relationship between the quadratic adjustment cost model that has become common in the literature on dynamic factor demand and the adjustment equations we have used in the empirical work reported in chapter 4. Details of our estimating procedures omitted from the text of chapter 4 are also described here.

Modeling Labor Adjustment

Structural models of employment and hours adjustment typically rest on the assumption that the cost of changing labor input is a quadratic function of the change in labor input (that is, adjustment costs are assumed to rise with the square of the rate of change in labor input). This assumption is needed to make the formal analysis of these models mathematically tractable.

Starting with this assumption, one can derive an expression for optimal employment today as a function of last period's employment, demand in the current period, and expected demand in future periods. The standard expression, in logarithmic form, is as follows:[1]

$$(4\text{-}1a) \quad \ln(N_t) = \mu\ln(N_{t-1}) + (1 - \mu)(1 - \mu\beta)\sum_{s=0}^{\infty}(\mu\beta)^s\ln(N_{t+s}^*)$$

where N_t is employment in period t, N_t^* is the quantity of labor that

_____

1. For a derivation of this model, see Sargent (1987, pp. 199-204.).

would be demanded in period t if there were no costs to employers associated with altering the level of employment, μ is a parameter to be estimated and β is the discount factor. Higher values of μ imply slower adjustment of labor to demand changes. In this model, the parameter μ is an increasing function of adjustment costs, but is not influenced by the persistence or magnitude of shocks to desired labor input. Under the assumptions made in this model's derivation, cross-country differences in μ reasonably can be ascribed to institutional differences between the two countries.

To empirically implement equation 4-1a it is necessary to specify the determinants of N_t^*. The empirical research on dynamic labor demand typically assumes that short-run changes in labor demand are largely attributable to changes in output and a process by which future expectations of output are generated. The usual derivation of the commonly used Koyck specification, in which current ln(employment) is regressed on lagged ln(employment) and current ln(output), assumes that businesses have static expectations about future demand.

Similar models can be developed assuming that businesses forecast future demand based on the past.[2] For example, suppose that desired employment varies directly with shipments:

$$(4\text{-}2a) \qquad \ln(N_t^*) = \Omega_0 + \Omega_1 t + \Omega_2 t^2 + \ln(S_t) + u_t$$

and that ln(shipments) follow a first-order autoregressive process:

$$(4\text{-}3a) \qquad \ln(S_t) = \phi_0 + \phi_1 t + \phi_2 t^2 + \rho \ln(S_{t-1}) + \omega_t$$

where S represents real shipments and ρ is a parameter that summarizes the persistence in shocks to $\ln(S)$. Using equations 4-2a and 4-3a to generate expected values for $\ln(N_{t+s}^*)$, and substituting these expected values into equation 4-1a yields:

$$(4\text{-}4a) \qquad \ln(N_t) = \alpha_0 + \alpha_1 t + \alpha_2 t^2 + \mu \ln(N_{t-1}) + \psi \ln(S_t) + v_t$$

where ψ is a parameter that depends upon μ, β, and ρ. Repeated substitution for the lagged $\ln(N)$ term in this expression produces the equivalent specification:

$$(4\text{-}5a) \qquad \ln(N_t) = \hat{\alpha}_0 + \hat{\alpha}_1 t + \hat{\alpha}_2 t^2 + \sum_{s=0}^{k} \psi \mu^s \ln(S_{t-s}) + \hat{v}_t$$

---

2. See Abraham and Houseman (1992).

where terms in ln(S) lagged more than k periods are assumed to have only a small effect on current ln(N) and have been dropped. Similar, somewhat more complicated, expressions can be derived for cases in which shipments follow a higher-order autoregressive process. In practice a second-order autoregression characterizes the German and U.S. shipments data adequately.

Although this class of model is attractive because the estimated value of μ has a structural interpretation, the assumption of quadratic adjustment costs, which enables this structural interpretation, imposes significant constraints on the path of employment adjustment. For example, following a one-time negative shock to demand, the quadratic adjustment cost specification implies that employment will gradually fall, but never quite reach its new demand level, N^*. The actual path of employment adjustment may be inconsistent with this implied path. If adjustment costs are not quadratic, the estimated value of μ may be a misleading measure of the speed of adjustment. We present some evidence concerning the applicability of the quadratic adjustment cost model in a recent paper.[3] Aggregate adjustment in a majority of German and U.S. industries appears to be reasonably characterized by the quadratic adjustment cost model, although there are some industries for which it performs poorly. The qualitative conclusions based on estimates of that model are similar to those we reach based on the models reported in the text.

The model shown in the text as equation 4-1 and repeated here:

$$\ln(N_t) = \Phi_0 + \Phi_1 t + \Phi_2 t^2 + \sum_{s=0}^{6} \theta_s \ln(S_{t-s}) + \epsilon_t$$

can be thought of as a more general version of 4-5a. Note that in both equations 4-1 and 4-5a, ln(N) is regressed on current and lagged values of ln(S), although without the assumption of quadratic adjustment costs, the estimated coefficients on the shipments terms in equation 4-1 have no structural interpretation. Nevertheless, equation 4-1 should provide useful descriptive evidence on differences in adjustment across countries and across industries within each country.

---

3. See Abraham and Houseman (1992).

Measures of the Persistence, Cyclicality, and Trend Growth of Shipments

Our measure of the persistence of shipments is equal to the coefficient on the lagged value of the logarithm of shipments from equation 4-3a. Cyclicality is measured as the standard deviation of the residual from a regression of the logarithm of shipments on a quadratic time trend:

$$(4\text{-}6a) \qquad \ln(S_t) = \delta_0 + \delta_1 t + \delta_2 t^2 + \pi_t.$$

The implied annual growth rate of shipments is calculated from the time trend coefficients in equation 4-6a at the midpoint of the 1974–84 period.

Estimating the Effects of Short Time on Hours Adjustment

We used published data on short time by industry to construct a series of short-time hours for nine German industries. Unfortunately, historical data on hours of short-time compensation paid are not available. The Federal Employment Service (Bundesanstalt für Arbeit), however, does publish monthly industry-level data on the number of workers collecting short-time payments, as well as annual industry-level data showing the percentages of workers on short time who had experienced a reduction in hours of zero to 25 percent, 25 to 50 percent, 50 to 75 percent, and 75 to 100 percent. While there has been great variation over time in the number of persons in each industry collecting short-time benefits, the distribution of workers by the size of their hours reduction has varied relatively little across industries and over time.

Using industry- and year-specific data on the distribution of individuals across hours reduction categories, we calculated an average proportional reduction in hours for persons on short time for each year during the 1974–84 period for each of the nine industries. Our calculations assume that hours reductions averaged 20 percent (one day a week) among workers in the first category, 40 percent (two days a week) among those in the second category, 60 percent (three days a week) among those in the third category, and 80 percent (four days a week) among those in the fourth category. Because the data on short time apply to all workers, while the data on hours of work used elsewhere in our analysis are for production workers only, we had to make an additional assumption about the distribution of short-time work between production and nonproduction workers to estimate the total number of short-time hours for production workers in each industry. We used two extreme assumptions to bound our estimates. The first is that short-time hours are distributed between production and nonproduction workers in proportion to their representation in the work force. The second assumption is that only production workers work short time. Based on these assumptions, we constructed two sets of monthly series showing the total number of short-time hours for production workers in each of nine industries.

Using these short-time hours series, we then adjusted the total production hours series for each industry to show what total hours would have been without short time. These adjusted hours series were used to estimate the production hours elasticities shown in table 4-11.

Estimating the Effects of Temporary Layoffs on Hours Adjustment

To estimate the contribution of temporary layoffs to labor adjustment in the United States, we used labor turnover data collected by the Bureau of Labor Statistics through 1981. Published statistics from the Labor Turnover Survey include monthly data on the total separations rate, the layoff rate, the quit rate, the total accessions rate, and the new hires rate for manufacturing industries. The published layoff statistics include temporary and permanent layoffs. Accessions that are not new hires consist primarily of recalls from temporary layoff, but they also include transfers from other establishments of the same firm.

To distinguish temporary from permanent layoffs, and also to identify the distribution of temporary layoff durations, we fit the following equation using seasonally adjusted monthly data for the time period 1971 to 1981 for each of the eleven manufacturing industries included in the previous analysis:

$$(4\text{-}7a) \quad ACCS_t - NEWHIRES_t = \gamma + \sum_{s=0}^{12} \eta_s LAYOFFS_{t-s} + \lambda_t$$

where $ACCS$ is the total accessions rate, $NEWHIRES$ is the new hire rate, $LAYOFFS$ is the layoff rate, and γ and the ηs are parameters to be estimated. The coefficient γ is intended to capture the average rate of interplant transfers; these are assumed not to vary systematically with previous periods' layoff rates. The η_s coefficients capture the average share of layoffs s periods ago that lead to recalls in the current period. The sum of the η_s coefficients equals the share of layoffs that are temporary ex post, assuming that recalls from layoffs that have lasted twelve months or more are negligible.[4]

The estimates from equation 4-7a suggest that a large share of layoffs in most industries is temporary rather than permanent. In the eleven industries for which we have data, the sum of the η_s's ranges from a low of 0.34 to a high of 0.71; the average share of layoffs that is temporary is about 50 percent.

We have used the estimates of equation 4-7a to investigate how employment would have adjusted had these temporary layoffs and recalls never occurred. Equation 4-7a can be used to determine how much lower each month's production worker separation rate and accession rate would have been in the absence of temporary layoffs and subsequent recalls under alternate assumptions about the distribution of temporary layoffs between production and nonproduction workers, all else remaining the same. Note that the percentage change in employment from one month to the next is approximately equal to the difference between the total accessions rate and the total separations rate. The information derived from equation 4-7a thus can be used to adjust the actual observed change in production employment for the effects of temporary layoffs. The fact that the percent change in total hours is approximately equal to the percent change in employment plus the percent change in average hours per person employed allows us to construct production hours series that show what hours would have been had there been no temporary layoffs and recalls. These adjusted numbers were then used to estimate the production hours elasticities reported in table 4-12.

---

4. The method used to distinguish between temporary and permanent layoff is essentially that used by Lilien (1980). We also experimented with allowing the ηs to vary with unemployment conditions; doing this did not add significantly to the explanatory power of our model.

Data Appendix to Chapter 4

THE GERMAN DATA on production employment, hours, and shipments come from a monthly employer survey conducted by the Federal Statistical Office (Statistisches Bundesamt). Production employment includes persons on the payroll as of the last day of the month. Total actual production worker hours during the month are also reported. These data are published monthly in *Fachserie 4: Produzierendes Gewerbe, Reihe 4.1.1: Beschäftigung, Umsatz und Energieversorgung der Unternehmen und Betriebe im Bergbau und im Verarbeitenden Gewerbe*, issued by the Statistisches Bundesamt. The German shipments data were deflated by a producer price index for basic industries, capital goods, consumer goods, or food and tobacco, as appropriate.

U.S. employment and hours data come from the Bureau of Labor Statistics' monthly Employment, Payroll, and Hours survey. Employment is reported for the payroll period including the twelfth of the month; average weekly paid hours per production worker are reported for the same payroll period. These data are published monthly in *Employment and Earnings*. U.S. shipments data were obtained from the Bureau of the Census's Manufacturers' Shipments, Inventories and Orders data set; these data are published in *Current Industrial Reports: Manufacturers' Shipments, Inventories and Orders*, which appears annually. The U.S. shipments data were deflated using either the durable goods or the nondurable goods producer price index.

Except for the producer price deflators, all relevant series were obtained on magnetic tape in unadjusted form and seasonally adjusted using the X-11 procedure in SAS. To account for the difference between the end-of-month reporting date for production employment in Germany and the midmonth date in the United States, we transformed the German production employment numbers, defining:

(4-1b) $$E'_t = (E_t + E_{t-1})/2.$$

These transformed numbers were used in all analyses, though making this adjustment had little effect on any of our estimates.

Another difference between the German and U.S. data series is that German employers are asked to report actual hours worked, while U.S. employers are asked to report paid hours. As described in the text, we have attempted to assess the importance of this difference in definition by using data from another German survey, the Verdiensterhebung in Industrie und Handel, which collected both actual and paid hours information quarterly from 1964 through 1972.

Neither country's data series are adjusted for the effect of strikes. We have added strike dummies to our estimating equations for the German automobile, primary metals, and printing industries in those quarters in which we knew that large strikes occurred and in the immediately following quarters. This has the effect of slightly reducing the estimated adjustment of hours worked to changes in output.

The monthly German shipments data turn out to be much noisier than the U.S. data. We suspect that this difference reflects differences in the procedures used to construct the German and U.S. series. The German shipments numbers are based on monthly reports filed by responding establishments, weighted and summed. The U.S. Bureau of the Census uses a "link relative" method to construct its shipments series. In essence, the estimated percentage change in shipments between the current and previous month based on data supplied by establishments that filed a report in both months is applied to last month's shipments number to arrive at the current month's number. If there is any month-to-month variation in the sample of reporting establishments, the U.S. procedures should produce a smoother series. The U.S. Bureau of the Census also takes great care to confirm the accuracy of the data supplied by reporting establishments, primarily through telephone contact with respondents whose numbers appear in any way to be anomalous. Because the monthly German shipments data were so noisy, we have averaged monthly observations to yield quarterly observations for both countries. This temporal aggregation of the data does not affect our qualitative findings in any important way.

Some important changes in the methods used to collect the German establishment data were introduced in 1977. The new survey universe includes craft (Handwerk) establishments and excludes establishments of enterprises with fewer than twenty employees. Under the new scheme, an establishment encompasses all activities conducted at a given site. The old survey excluded craft establishments and establishments with fewer than ten employees. Under the old scheme, an establishment encompassed the industrial part of activities conducted at a given site. Finally, a new industry classification scheme was introduced at the same time that the survey methods were altered. All of these changes are described in greater detail by Arnim Sobotschinski.[1]

The Statistisches Bundesamt has extended the data series constructed on the new reporting basis back to 1970 for two-digit industries. Data constructed on the old basis are available for the 1962–76 period. The analyses shown in tables 4-3 and 4-4 compare employment and hours adjustment over the 1962–72 and 1974–84 periods. Before conducting these analyses, we examined the 1970–76 data constructed on the new and old bases. Industries for which the methodological revisions just described appeared to have affected the behavior of the data were deleted from all analyses.

The models estimated for table 4-6 and table 4-7 include measures of the persistence of shipments, the cyclicality of shipments, the proportion of production workers who are female, and the share of labor costs in value added for each of thirty-one disaggregated German industries and forty-nine disaggregated U.S. industries. The first two of these variables were constructed using the monthly data on real shipments for each country already described. For Germany, data on the female share of production employment were taken from *Kostenstruktur der Unternehmen im Bergbau, Grundstoff- und Produktionsgütergewerbe 1977*, table 7; *Kostenstruktur der Unternehmen im Investitionsgüter produzierenden Gewerbe 1977*, table 7; and *Kostenstruktur der Unternehmen im Verbrauchsgüter produzierenden Gewerbe und im Nahrungs- und Genußmittelgewerbe 1977*, table 7, all published by the Statistisches Bundesamt. Labor's share in value added was computed based on data reported in the 1980 *Statistisches Jahrbuch*, p. 162, also published by the Statistisches Bundesamt. The female share of production employment was calculated for the United States using a merged annual Current Population Survey data file for 1983 and labor's share in value added was computed based

1. See Sobotschinski (1976).

on data from the *Census of Manufactures, 1977, General Summary*, chapter 2, Industry Statistics, table 1 and table 2.

The numbers used in the preparation of figure 4-2 equal the total number of workers collecting short-time benefits expressed as a percentage of total industrial employment. Annual data on the number of workers collecting short-time benefits were taken from *Amtliche Nachrichten der Bundesanstalt für Arbeit – Jahreszahlen* (various issues), published by the Federal Employment Service (Bundesanstalt für Arbeit), and from *Arbeits- und Sozialstatistik – Hauptergebnisse 1990*, published by the Minister for Labor and Social Affairs (Bundesminister für Arbeit und Sozialordnung). Data on industrial employment were obtained from *Lange Reihen zur Wirtschaftsentwicklung* (various years), published by the Statistisches Bundesamt, and from *Arbeits- und Sozialstatistik – Hauptergebnisse 1990*. Since the only consistent published series on short-time benefit receipt includes all recipients, not just industrial sector recipients, our figures slightly overstate the true percentages of industrial workers collecting benefits. This should not seriously distort either their level or time pattern, since industrial workers typically account for 95 percent or more of persons receiving short-time benefits, and this share varies little from year to year.

The analysis summarized in table 4-10 makes use of monthly data on the number of workers in each industry collecting short-time payments and annual data on the distribution of workers in each industry according to the percentage reduction in their hours of work. All of these numbers were taken from *Amtliche Nachrichten der Bundesanstalt für Arbeit – Jahreszahlen* (various issues).

The monthly data on total accessions, new hires, and layoffs by industry used for table 4-11 were collected by the Bureau of Labor Statistics as part of its Labor Turnover Survey program until 1981 and were obtained directly from that agency.

Data Appendix to Chapter 5

THE DATA SOURCES for the empirical work on production and non-production employment adjustment reported in table 5-1 and table 5-2 are the same as those underlying the empirical work in chapter 4, described in appendix B.

The numbers and analysis reported in tables 5-3 through 5-6 and figures 5-1 and 5-2 require data on employment, labor force, and population by detailed age group and sex. The demographic data for Germany come from the Mikrozensus, an annual household survey conducted in the spring of each year. These data are reported annually in *Fachserie 1: Bevölkerung und Erwerbstätigkeit, Reihe 4.1.1: Stand und Entwicklung der Erwerbstätigkeit*, published by the Federal Statistical Office (Statistisches Bundesamt). We obtained the relevant time series directly from the Statistisches Bundesamt on magnetic disk. While these data include military personnel from 1972 onwards, the pre-1972 data refer to the civilian population only. We used the civilian employment numbers with data on total employment taken from various issues of the *Statistisches Jahrbuch*, also published by the Statistisches Bundesamt, to identify the number of military personnel in each age/sex group in each year prior to 1972. We then added those numbers to the civilian employment, labor force, and population numbers for those years supplied on magnetic disk.

For the German by age group demographic data, the method used to determine an individual's age was changed in the early 1970s, causing a break in the series. In the years before 1972, age was calculated based solely on an individual's birth year. Beginning in 1972, age was calculated using information on the individual's actual month of birth. In light of this problem, when running the equations that underlie table 5-5, we omitted observations for the years 1972 and 1973.

Demographic data for the United States come from the monthly Current Population Survey, which like the Mikrozensus is a household survey, and are published by the Bureau of Labor Statistics in *Employment and Earnings*. The U.S. data are on a civilian population basis.

The unemployment and labor force concepts used in reported statistics based on the Mikrozensus are somewhat different than those used for the Current Population Survey. The German unemployment numbers count as unemployed persons who say they are available for work, irrespective of whether they have actively searched for a job. Job seekers not currently available for work—most importantly students—also are counted as unemployed. Persons due to start a new job are counted as out of the labor force, and persons on temporary layoff are counted as employed. The latter group are, however, of trivial importance. In contrast, the U.S. unemployment figures include job seekers currently available for work, plus persons due to start a new job within thirty days and persons on temporary layoff. People who say they are available for work but who have not actively searched for a job in the past four weeks are not counted as unemployed. The German labor force numbers include unpaid family workers working less than fifteen hours a week; the U.S. labor force numbers do not. In addition, whereas the German labor force numbers include all military personnel, the U.S. numbers include only those who are domestically based.

The construction of the estimates reported in table 5-5 and table 5-6 also require data on output. The GDP data for Germany come from the OECD *Economic Outlook*. The GNP data for the United States come from the *Survey of Current Business*.

The estimates of male and female employment by industry for Germany underlying the analysis reported in table 5-7 were constructed using the data on production and nonproduction employment described earlier in conjunction with quarterly data from another survey on the gender composition of employment. Data on the share of blue-collar workers who are female come from Statistisches Bundesamt, *Fachserie 16; Löhne und Gehälter, Reihe 2.1; Arbeiterverdienste in der Industrie*. Data on the share of white-collar workers who are female come from Statistisches Bundesamt, *Fachserie 16; Löhne und Gehälter, Reihe 2.2; Angestelltenverdienste in Industrie und Handel*. The U.S. data on male and female employment by industry underlying table 5-8 come from the same source as the employment data used for the work reported in chapter 4.

The unemployment rate data reported in table 5-9 are official statistics based on registrations with the employment service reported in *Amtliche Nachrichten der Bundesanstalt für Arbeit – Jahreszahlen* (various years), published by the Federal Employment Service (Bundesanstalt für Arbeit). The data on the net migration of foreigners used in figure 5-3 were taken from *Strukturdaten über Ausländer in der Bundesrepublik Deutschland* (1983) and *Lange Reihen zur Wirtschaftsentwicklung* (various years), both published by the Statistisches Bundesamt. The proportions reported in figure 5-4 are based on social security statistics reported in *Amtliche Nachrichten der Bundesanstalt für Arbeit – Jahreszahlen* (various years).

References

Abraham, Katharine G., and Susan N. Houseman. 1992. "Employment Security and Labor Adjustment: A Comparison of West Germany and the United States." Working Paper. University of Maryland.

Abraham, Katharine G., and James L. Medoff. 1984. "Length of Service and Layoffs in Union and Nonunion Work Groups." *Industrial and Labor Relations Review* 38 (October):87–97.

———. 1985. "Length of Service and Promotions in Union and Nonunion Work Groups." *Industrial and Labor Relations Review* 38 (April):408–20.

Addison, John, and Pedro Portugal. 1987. "The Effect of Advance Notification of Plant Closings on Unemployment." *Industrial and Labor Relations Review* 41 (October):3–16.

Blanchard, Olivier J. 1989. *Two Tools for Analyzing Unemployment.* Working Paper 3168. Cambridge, Mass.: National Bureau of Economic Research.

Blanchard, Olivier J., and Lawrence H. Summers. 1988. "Hysteresis and the European Unemployment Problem." In *Unemployment, Hysteresis and the Natural Rate Hypothesis*, edited by Rod Cross, 306–63. London: Basil Blackwell.

Blanchflower, David G., and Lisa M. Lynch. 1991. "Training at Work: A Comparison of U.S. and British Youths." Paper prepared for the NBER/CEP conference on International Comparisons of Private Sector Training. London.

Boyd, Monica. 1976. "Immigration Policies and Trends: A Comparison of Canada and the United States." *Demography* 13 (February):83–104.

Brandes, Wolfgang, Wolfgang Meyer, and Edwin Schudlich. 1991. "Pay Classification Systems: National Monograph for Germany." Paper prepared for the ILO Research Project on Pay Classification in Industrialised Countries. Geneva.

Briggs, Vernon M. 1986. "The 'Albatross' of Immigration Reform: Temporary

Worker Policy in the United States." *International Migration Review* 20 (Winter):995–1019.

Bruche, Gert, and Bernd Reissert. 1984. "Manpower and Regional Adjustment Policies: The Case of West Germany." Paper prepared for a study on the Adjustment Component of Trade Policy, conducted by the Institute for International Economics. Washington.

Büchtemann, Christoph F. 1989. "More Jobs through Less Employment Protection? Lessons from an Evaluation of the West German 'Employment Promotion Act 1985'." Paper prepared for the 1989 meeting of the European Association of Labour Economists (EALE). Turin.

———. 1990. "Employment Protection and 'De-Regulation': The West German Experience." Paper prepared for the ILO/IILS/WZB international conference on Workers' Protection and Labor Market Dynamics. Berlin.

Büchtemann, Christoph F., and Sigrid Quack. 1989. "'Bridges' or 'Traps': Nonstandard Employment in the Federal Republic of Germany." In *Precarious Jobs in Labour Market Regulation: The Growth of Atypical Employment in Western Europe*, edited by Gerry Rodgers and Janine Rodgers, 109–48. Geneva: International Institute for Labour Studies.

Bundesanstalt für Arbeit. 1991. *Arbeitsmarkt 1990–Strukturanalyse anhand ausgewählter Bestands- und Bewegungsdaten.* Nürnberg.

Burda, Michael C., and Jeffrey D. Sachs. 1987. *Institutional Aspects of High Unemployment in the Federal Republic of Germany.* Working Paper 2241. Cambridge, Mass.: National Bureau of Economic Research.

Burtless, Gary. 1987. "Jobless Pay and High European Unemployment." In *Barriers to European Growth: A Transatlantic View*, edited by Robert Z. Lawrence and Charles L. Schultze, 105–74. Brookings.

Carter, Susan B., and Richard Sutch. 1991. "Sticky Wages, Short Weeks, and 'Fairness': The Response of Connecticut Manufacturing Firms to the Depression of 1893–94." Paper prepared for presentation to the McGill University Conference on Labour Market Evolution. Montreal.

Casey, Bernard. 1986. "The Dual Apprenticeship System and the Recruitment and Retention of Young Persons in West Germany." *British Journal of Industrial Relations* 24 (March):63–81.

Chiswick, Barry R. 1988. *Illegal Aliens: Their Employment and Employers.* Kalamazoo, Mich: W. E. Upjohn Institute for Employment Research.

Clark, Kim B., and Lawrence H. Summers. 1981. "Demographic Differences in Cyclical Employment Variation." *Journal of Human Resources* 16 (Winter):61–79.

Commission of the European Communities. 1984. *European Women in Paid Employment, 1984.* Luxembourg: Office for Official Publications of the European Communities.

Däubler-Gmelin, Herta. 1980. "Equal Employment Opportunity for Women in West Germany Today." In *Equal Employment Policy for Women: Strategies in the United States, Canada, and Western Europe*, edited by Ronnie Steinberg Ratner, 329–49. Temple University Press.

Deutschmann, Christoph. 1982. "Produktion, Technischer Fortschritt, und Beschäftigung." SAMF Arbeitspapier 1982–3.

Ehrenberg, Ronald G., and George H. Jakubson. 1988. *Advance Notice Provisions in Plant Closing Legislation*. Kalamazoo, Mich: W. E. Upjohn Institute for Employment Research.

Falke, Josef, and others. 1981. *Kündigungspraxis und Kündigungsschutz in der Bundesrepublik Deutschland*. Bonn: Bundesminister für Arbeit und Sozialordnung.

Federal Minister of Labor and Social Affairs. 1980. *Co-determination in the Federal Republic of Germany*. Bonn.

Flaim, Paul O., and Ellen Sehgal. 1985. "Displaced Workers of 1979–83: How Well Have They Fared?" *Monthly Labor Review* 108 (June):3–16.

Flanagan, Robert J. 1987. "Labor Market Behavior and European Economic Growth." In *Barriers to European Growth: A Transatlantic View*, edited by Robert Z. Lawrence and Charles L. Schultze, 175–229. Brookings.

Flanagan, Robert J., David W. Soskice, and Lloyd Ulman. 1983. *Unionism, Economic Stabilization and Incomes Policies: European Experience*. Brookings.

Flechsenhar, Hans Rolf. 1980. *Kurzarbeit als Massnahme der betrieblichen Anpassung*. Frankfurt am Main: Verlag Harri Deutsch.

Franz, Wolfgang. 1986. "Match or Mismatch? The Anatomy of Structural/Frictional Unemployment in Germany: A Theoretical and Empirical Investigation." Working Paper. University of Stuttgart.

———. 1991. "Match and Mismatch in the German Labour Market." *Mismatch and Labour Mobility*, edited by Fiorella Padoa Schioppa, 105-35. Cambridge University Press.

Freeman, Richard B. 1989. "The Changing Status of Unionism around the World: Some Emerging Patterns." In *Organized Labor at the Crossroads*, edited by Wei-Chiao Huang, 111–37. Kalamazoo, Mich: W. E. Upjohn Institute for Employment Research.

Gavin, Michael K. 1986. *Labor Market Rigidities and Unemployment: The Case of Severance Costs*. Washington: Federal Reserve Board, Division of International Finance.

Grais, Bernard. 1983. *Lay-offs and Short-Time Working in Selected OECD Countries*. Paris: Organization for Economic Cooperation and Development.

Hamermesh, Daniel S. 1978. "Unemployment Insurance, Short-Time Compensation, and the Workweek." In *Work Time and Employment*, National Commission for Manpower Policy, 231–64. Special Report 28. Washington.

———. 1989. "Labor Demand and the Structure of Adjustment Costs." *American Economic Review* 79 (September):674–89.

Hamilton, Stephen F. 1990. *Apprenticeship for Adulthood: Preparing Youth for the Future*. Free Press.

Hemmer, Edmund. 1988. *Sozialplanpraxis in der Bundesrepublik: Eine empirische Untersuchung*. Köln: Deutscher Instituts-Verlag GmbH.

Hilton, Margret. 1991. "Shared Training: Learning from Germany." *Monthly Labor Review* 114 (March):33–37.

Houseman, Susan N. 1988. "Shorter Working Time and Job Security: Labor Adjustment in the Steel Industry." In *Employment, Unemployment and Labor Utilization*, edited by Robert A. Hart, 64–85. London: Unwin Hyman.

———. 1990. "The Equity and Efficiency of Job Security: Contrasting Perspectives on Collective Dismissal Laws in Western Europe." In *New Developments in the Labor Market: Toward a New Institutional Paradigm*, edited by Katharine Abraham and Robert McKersie, 185–210. MIT Press.

———. 1991. *Industrial Restructuring with Job Security: The Case of European Steel*. Harvard University Press.

Houseman, Susan N., and Katharine G. Abraham. 1990. "The Distributional Effects of Employment Adjustment Practices in Japan versus the United States." Working Paper. Kalamazoo, Mich.: W. E. Upjohn Institute for Employment Research.

Howe, Wayne J. 1990. "Labor Market Dynamics and Trends in Male and Female Unemployment." *Monthly Labor Review* 113 (November):3–12.

Hunt, Jennifer. 1992. "The Effect of Unemployment Compensation on Unemployment Duration in Germany." Working Paper. Harvard University.

International Labour Organization. 1990. *Year Book of Labour Statistics 1989/90*. Geneva.

Jacobs, Klaus, Martin Kohli, and Martin Rein. 1987. "Early Exit from the Labor Force in Germany." Working Paper. Presented at meetings on Early Exit from the Labor Force. Paris.

Jacoby, Sanford M. 1985. *Employing Bureaucracy: Managers, Unions, and the Transformation of Work in American Industry, 1900–1945*. Columbia University Press.

Katz, Lawrence F., and Bruce D. Meyer. 1990. "Unemployment Insurance, Recall Expectations, and Unemployment Outcomes." *Quarterly Journal of Economics* 105 (November):973–1002.

Kerachsky, Stuart, and others. 1985. "An Evaluation of Short-Time Compensation Programs." Report prepared for the Office of Strategic Planning and Policy Development, U.S. Department of Labor, Occasional Paper 86-4.

Köhler, Christoph, and Werner Sengenberger. 1983. *Konjunktur und Personalanpassung: Betriebliche Beschäftingungspolitik in der deutschen und amerikanischen Automobilindustrie*. Frankfurt: Campus Verlag.

Kühlewind, Gerhard. 1986. "Beschäftigung und Ausgliederung älterer Arbeitnehmer." *Mitteilungen aus der Arbeitsmarkt- und Berufsforschung* (February):209–32.

Langley, Monica, and Gerald F. Seib. 1988. "Trade Bill Conferees Expected to

Clear Rule on Advance Notice of Plant Closings," *Wall Street Journal*, March 29, p. 3.

Lawrence, Robert Z., and Charles L. Schultze, eds. 1987. *Barriers to European Growth: A Transatlantic View*. Brookings.

Leigh, Duane E. 1989. *Assisting Displaced Workers: Do the States Have a Better Idea?* Kalamazoo, Mich.: W. E. Upjohn Institute for Employment Research.

Lilien, David M. 1980. "The Cyclical Pattern of Temporary Layoffs in United States Manufacturing." *Review of Economics and Statistics* 62 (February):24–31.

Lindbeck, Assar. 1985. "What Is Wrong with the West European Economies?" *World Economy* 8 (June):153–70.

Medoff, James L. 1979. "Layoffs and Alternatives under Trade Unions in U.S. Manufacturing." *American Economic Review* 69 (June):380–95.

Medoff, James L., and Katharine G. Abraham. 1980. "Experience, Performance and Earnings." *Quarterly Journal of Economics* 94 (December):703–36.

———. 1981. "Are Those Paid More Really More Productive?" *Journal of Human Resources* 16 (Spring):186–216.

Meisel, Harry. 1984. "The Pioneers: STC in the Federal Republic of Germany." In *Short-Time Compensation: A Formula for Work Sharing*, edited by Ramelle MaCoy and Martin J. Morand, 53–60. Pergamon Press.

Meyers, Frederick. 1964. *Ownership of Jobs: A Comparative Study*. University of California at Los Angeles, Institute of Industrial Relations.

Münch, Joachim. 1991. *Vocational Training in the Federal Republic of Germany*. 3d ed. Berlin: European Centre for the Development of Vocational Training.

National Commission on Unemployment Compensation. 1980. *Unemployment Compensation: Final Report*. Washington: Government Printing Office.

National Foundation for Unemployment Compensation and Workers' Compensation. 1991. *Highlights of State Unemployment Compensation Laws*. Washington.

Nemirow, Martin. 1984. "Short-Time Compensation: Some Policy Considerations." In *Short-Time Compensation: A Formula for Work Sharing*, edited by Ramelle MaCoy and Martin Morand, 158–82. Pergamon Press.

Nickell, S. J. 1986. "Dynamic Models of Labour Demand." In *Handbook of Labor Economics*, volume I, edited by O. Ashenfelter and R. Layard, 473–522. Amsterdam: Elsevier Science Publishers BV.

Organization for Economic Cooperation and Development. 1985. *OECD Economic Surveys 1984/1985: Germany*. Paris.

———. 1986. *Flexibility in the Labour Market: The Current Debate*. Paris.

———. 1987. *OECD Economic Surveys 1986/1987: Germany*. Paris.

———. 1990. *OECD Economic Outlook* 47 (June). Paris.

Osterman, Paul. 1988. *Employment Futures: Reorganization, Dislocation, and Public Policy*. Oxford University Press.

Paqué, Karl-Heinz. undated. "Labour Market Contracts and Institutions: The Case of Germany." Working Paper. University of Kiel.

Piore, Michael J. 1986. "Perspectives on Labor Market Flexibility." *Industrial Relations* 25 (Spring):146–66.

Podgursky, Michael, and Paul Swaim. 1987. "Duration of Joblessness following Job Displacement." *Industrial Relations* 26 (Fall):213–26.

Ruhm, Christopher J. 1989. "Advance Notice and Postdisplacement Joblessness." Paper presented at the Universities Research Conference on Labor Markets in the 1990s, sponsored by the National Bureau of Economic Research. Cambridge, Mass.

Sachs, Jeffrey D. 1979. "Wages, Profits, and Macroeconomic Adjustment: A Comparative Study." *Brookings Papers on Economic Activity* 2:269–319.

———. 1983. "Real Wages and Unemployment in the OECD Countries." *Brookings Papers on Economic Activity* 1:255-304.

Samborn, Randall. 1990. "A Fizzling Time Bomb." *National Law Journal*, January 22:1.

Sargent, Thomas J. 1987. *Macroeconomic Theory.* 2d ed. Boston: Academic Press.

Schettkat, Ronald. 1992. *The Labor Market Dynamics of Economic Restructuring: The United States and Germany in Transition.* Praeger.

Schultze, Charles L. 1987. "Real Wages, Real Wage Aspirations, and Unemployment in Europe." In *Barriers to European Growth: A Transatlantic View,* edited by Robert Z. Lawrence and Charles L. Schultze, 230–302. Brookings.

Seitchik, Adam, and Jeffrey Zornitsky. 1989. *From One Job to the Next: Worker Adjustment in a Changing Labor Market.* Kalamazoo, Mich.: W. E. Upjohn Institute for Employment Research.

Sengenberger, Werner. 1985. "Employment Security: Redundancy Arrangements and Practices in West Germany." Report prepared for the Organization for Economic Cooperation and Development. Paris.

Sobotschinski, Arnim. 1976. "Die Neuordnung der Statistik des Produzierenden Gewerbes." *Wirtschaft und Statistik* (July):405–12.

Soltwedel, Rüdiger. 1988. "Employment Problems in West Germany—The Role of Institutions, Labor Law, and Government Intervention." In *Stabilization Policies and Labor Markets,* 153–220. Carnegie-Rochester Conference Series on Public Policy 28. Amsterdam.

Statistisches Bundesamt. 1978. *Fachserie 1: Bevölkerung und Erwerbstätigkeit, Reihe 4.1, Stand und Entwicklung der Erwerbstätigkeit.* Stuttgart: W. Kohlhammer GmbH.

———. 1979. *Statistisches Jahrbuch.* Stuttgart: W. Kohlhammer GmbH.

———. 1987. *Statistisches Jahrbuch.* Stuttgart: W. Kohlhammer GmbH.

Streeck, Wolfgang. 1987. "Industrial Relations in West Germany: Agenda for Change." Discussion Paper IIM/LMP 87-5. Berlin: Wissenschaftszentrum Berlin für Sozialforschung, Forschungsschwerpunkt Arbeitsmarkt und Beschäftigung.

Swaim, Paul, and Michael Podgursky. 1990. "Advance Notice and Job Search: The Value of an Early Start." *Journal of Human Resources* 25 (Spring): 147–78.

U.S. Congress. Office of Technology Assessment. 1990. *Worker Training: Competing in the New International Economy*. Report OTA-ITE-457. Washington.

U.S. Department of Labor. Bureau of International Labor Affairs. 1989. *The Effects of Immigration on the U.S. Economy and Labor Market*. Immigration Policy and Research Report 1. Washington.

U.S. Department of Labor. Bureau of Labor Statistics. 1981. *Characteristics of Major Collective Bargaining Agreements, January 1, 1980*. Bulletin 2095. Washington.

———. 1982. *Labor Force Statistics Derived from the Current Population Survey: A Databook, Volume I*. Bulletin 2096. Washington.

———. 1991. *Underlying Data for Indexes of Output per Hour, Hourly Compensation, and Unit Labor Costs in Manufacturing, Twelve Industrial Countries, 1950–1989*. Washington.

———. 1992. *Comparative Labor Force Statistics, Ten Countries, 1959–91*. Washington.

U.S. Department of Labor. Employment and Training Administration. undated. *Unemployment Insurance Financial Data*. ET Handbook 394. Washington.

U.S. General Accounting Office. 1986. *Dislocated Workers: Extent of Business Closures, Layoffs, and the Public and Private Response*. Briefing Report to the Honorable Lloyd Bentsen, United States Senate. GAO/HRD-86-116BC. July 1.

Vroman, Wayne. 1989. "Experience Rating in Unemployment Insurance: Some Current Issues." U.S. Department of Labor, Employment and Training Administration, Unemployment Insurance Occasional Paper 89-6.

———. 1990. "An Essay on Short Time Compensation." Working Paper. Urban Institute. Washington.

———. 1992. "Short-Time Compensation in the U.S., Germany and Belgium." Unpublished Paper.

Vroman, Wayne, and Douglas Wissoker. 1990. "Alternatives for Managing Production Cutbacks." Report prepared for the National Commission for Employment Policy. Washington.

Warnken, Jürgen, and Gerd Ronning. 1990. "Technological Change and Employment Structures." In *Technological Change and Employment: Innovation in the German Economy*, edited by Ronald Schettkat and Michael Wagner, 215–53. New York: de Gruyter.

Weiler, Paul. 1983. "Promises to Keep: Securing Workers' Rights to Self-Organization under the NLRA." *Harvard Law Review* 96 (June): 1769–1827.

Weiss, Manfred. 1986. "F. R. of Germany." In "Restructuring Labour in the

Enterprise: Law and Practice in France, F. R. of Germany, Italy, Sweden, and the United Kingdom," edited by R. Blanpain, 25–52. *Bulletin of Comparative Labour Relations*.

———. 1987. *Labour Law and Industrial Relations in the Federal Republic of Germany*. Boston: Kluwer Law and Taxation Publishers.

Index